HOSPITALITY MANAGEMENT

Acknowledgements

The Publishers would like to thank the following for permission to reproduce material in this volume:

Horwarth Consulting for 'Statistical Information', 'Operational Information' and 'Market Information'; ICC Information Group for 'Key Ratios'.

Every effort has been made to trace and acknowledgement ownership of copyright. The publishers will be glad to make suitable arrangements with any copyright holders whom it has not been possible to contact.

a case study approach

HOSPITALITY
management

John Lennon
Mark Peet

Hodder & Stoughton
LONDON SYDNEY AUCKLAND TORONTO

To Mark, a good friend.

Typeset by Taurus Graphics, Abingdon, Oxon.
Printed in Great Britain for Hodder and Stoughton
Educational and Academic, a division of Hodder and
Stoughton Ltd, Mill Road, Dunton Green, Sevenoaks, Kent
by Thomson Litho Ltd, East Kilbride.

Contents

Introduction

This book has been written for use by students and lecturers across the range of hotel, catering and related management courses. It attempts to integrate themes drawn from core management subjects such as finance, marketing and human resource management. The ten case studies presented vary in complexity and are based on operational scenarios drawn from a number of sectors within the hospitality industry. Together with a section on case study technique, the book will be suitable for students undertaking the following courses: HCIMA certificate and diploma, BTEC and SCOTVEC higher diploma, degree and postgraduate courses.

The case study approach has been employed for some time as a teaching tool in both the educational environment and in the industrial situation. The value of such an approach is clear: it fosters the development of analytical skills consistent with real business situations; it encourages participants to contribute to group discussion; and it helps to create an awareness that issues and problems in the business situation are seldom monocausal or simple in their solution.

However, there are some difficulties with the case study approach. These can range from how to identify information relevant to given issues; or how to identify cause/effect relationships; or how to offer realistic suggestions for alternative courses of action. The authors believe that *their* approach has acknowledged some of the common difficulties faced by respondents. Part One of this book attempts to overcome some of these by providing suggestions to the approach, analysis and response of case studies. It covers those areas the authors have, from experience, found most problematic for respondents.

The cases in Part Two provide a number of realistic operational scenarios which demand the integration of a range of subject areas from within hotel and catering management courses. The authors take the view that case studies become more realistic, and hence more useful, if they are discussed in context with information presented elsewhere. Thus, reading from appropriate external sources is encouraged as it allows you to place the case scenario in the *real* world.

The text is accompanied by a tutor's manual containing the authors' suggestions for case study responses. These are by no means the *right* answers — these do not exist. However, the manual has been written to assist both tutor and student to arrive at *possible* courses of action and to stimulate discussion.

Finally, in anticipation of the possible criticism that many of the case studies focus on hotel scenarios, the authors would like to make to following points:

- Most of the cases presented are drawn from consultancy work in which hotels have predominated. The value of using such realistic cases was seen to far outweigh a more wide-ranging, but somewhat unbalanced, spread of scenarios.
- Many of the problems and solutions found in hotel scenarios have relevance and application in other settings, and so should not be regarded as 'hotel bias' or 'hotel exclusive'.

Using this text

As you will have noted, this book is divided into two parts. Part One is a guide to case study analyses and responses and the first chapter introduces you to the usefulness of case studies and gives a framework for your responses. This is followed by a chapter on financial analysis, which attempts to develop your awareness of common parameters and measurements of business performance. A worked example comparing different types of catering establishments is included to demonstrate techniques and formulas that can be used. This chapter is given emphasis because students often have difficulty with financial concepts.

A format for writing your report is then presented. It is hoped that this will allow you to clarify your thoughts and ideas and adopt a response that will be logical and coherent. Such a response will be strengthened by the use of external reference material and guidance is given on the use of such material. The use of management reports and the adoption of the Harvard system of referencing adds emphasis to the format's simplicity and relevance — the narrative style of the essay is unsuitable and more complex styles of referencing are unnecessary.

Part One ends with a suggested bibliography. The list is by no means exhaustive but provides an alternative to the many text books which offer only limited assistance with case study exercises.

Part Two contains the case studies with questions. It commences with a worked example: this case is designed to be tutor led and should serve to focus your thinking on the importance of finance in all aspects of hospitality management. The remaining nine cases present a variety of scenarios, and are intended to be the basis for an interactive approach to hospitality management learning.

J. J. Lennon
M. Peet
Edinburgh May 1990

PART ONE

*A Guide to Case Study Analyses
and Responses*

1 The usefulness of case studies

The Value of Case Studies

The case study method fulfils a number of learning objectives in that it:

- Presents real problems to individuals with different experiences.

- Develops analytical skills in decision making under conditions of imperfect knowledge.

- Develops flexibility of thinking.

- Draws attention to the probable complexity of these apparently simple problems.

- Provides a means of applying theory to a practical situation.

- Helps individuals to view a business in perspective and demonstration that a successful business depends upon the effective contribution and interaction of all functions.

- Reveals personal values governing decisions.

- Compares decisions previously made in similar situations.

The Limitation of Case Studies

Case studies are often criticised on the grounds that they do not present all the facts in a situation. However, in the workplace, access to all the facts is seldom possible and reasonable assumptions may have to be made. Similarly, in case study analysis one has to make reasonable assumptions about causes and effects. If this is done, you must indicate what assumptions have been made and provide reasoned arguments for making them.

Some case analysis techniques argue that information outside the case should not be used. In the context of this book it is suggested that *any* information that provides a more realistic approach should be considered.

Case study technique

One of management's fundamental tasks is to make and implement decisions. Many such decisions are made when access to relevant information is limited or when uncertainty exists in the market place. In addition, time constraints will sometimes dictate a particular course of action being taken rather than another. The making of a decision can be broken down into several stages:

1. Examination of a situation to identify the issues or problems.

2. Formulation and evaluation of alternative courses of action and methods of implementation.

3. Implementation of the chosen course of action.

A case study uses a business situation as a basis for learning the process of decision making. The aim is to create a situation as near to the realities of business life as possible and often the case study is drawn from the history of a real business. Questions will normally focus on operational analysis in the light of the information given in the case study and appropriate research.

Problem/Issue Identification

As there is no standard response to all of the problems and opportunities that face the hospitality manager, there is no standard response to the cases contained in this text. However, one can make use of a number of techniques of analysis which can be applied to varying degrees to a wide range of problems. Once the problems and issues within a case are discovered, then more reliable decisions can be made about the action to be taken.

A common technique utilised in management and business texts is SWOT analysis. This technique will not provide answers to operating issues but will identify relevant problems, from which more informed decisions can be made. Essentially, SWOT analysis provides the student with four key titles under which analysis and potential of a given case can be examined. The acronym stands for: Strengths, Weaknesses, Opportunities, Threats.

Each one of these main areas requires some development to enable students to make and carry out detailed and specific analysis of case scenarios. It is important to note that 'Strengths' and 'Weaknesses' emerge from the firm's *internal* circumstances, while 'Opportunities' and 'Threats' exist in the firm's *external* environment. There are grey areas between the two sets of circumstances, but an important distinction to take into account is that internal issues are, to an extent, within the control of the firm, while external issues are largely beyond such control.

Strengths

A strength is essentially a competitive advantage that exists *within* the firm. It may take the form of a staff or management skill, a unique resource, powerful brand image, market dominance or an advantageous buyer/supplier relationship.

Weaknesses

A weakness is a competitive disadvantage that exists *within* the firm. It can be a deficiency in staff or management skills, resources, image, market standing or buyer/supplier relationship.

Opportunities

An opportunity is a favourable situation in a firm's environment. Opportunities can be maximised to ensure greater sales and higher profitability. Examples of opportunities include a growth in market potential or an emergence of new market segments, changes in legal regulations governing trading, technological advances and so on.

Threats

A threat is an unfavourable aspect of the firm's environment. Threats can potentially affect the firm's ability to operate within the given market situation. Threats can take the form of the emergence of competition, a decline in market potential or new legal restrictions imposed on trading.

The Problem/Issue Identification Matrix

While SWOT analysis is not the only technique available to assist managers to identify business issues, the authors have adopted the technique because of its simplicity and clarity. However, it has been developed further, to incorporate a problem/issue identification matrix.

The SWOT problem/issue identification matrix can be used as a systematic technique for case study analysis. There is a necessity to identify and classify the major and related problems; it is rarely sufficient to identify a central problem as monocausal or simply as a symptom of bad management. In the context of this book, common issues in the hospitality management field are located in the following areas:

- Operations

- Marketing

- Personnel

- Finance.

Problem/Issue Identification Matrix — The Internal Environment

	Strengths	**Weaknesses**
Operations		
	Expert management	Ineffective management
	Highly-skilled staff	Untrained staff
	Material cost advantage	High cost of materials
	Economies of scale	No access to economies of scale
	Efficient use of technology	Dated technology
	Effective service systems	Ineffective service systems
	Good brand image	Poor brand image
	Strong market for product portfolio	Weak market for product portfolio
Marketing		
	Skilled marketing department	Ineffective marketing department
	Effective sales training	Ineffective sales training
	Imaginative/efficient sales promotion	Ineffective sales promotion
	Knowledge of consumer demands	Lack of consumer research
	Ability to gain access to market	Barriers to entry to market
	Extensive distribution network	Restricted distribution network
	Effective product portfolio	Narrow product portfolio
	Product/service expansion potential	Limit to product/service potential
	Pricing flexibility	Inflexible pricing
	Brand loyalty	Lack of brand loyalty
	Good service image	Poor service image

	Strengths	**Weaknesses**

Personnel

Strengths	**Weaknesses**
Well trained staff	Poorly trained staff
Good employee relations	Poor labour relations
High labour retention rates	High labour turnover
Low or competitive labour costs	High labour costs
Low absenteeism	High absenteeism
Effective use of productivity incentives	Little use of productivity incentives
Effective training and development policy	Poor training and development policy

Financial

Strengths	**Weaknesses**
Skilled finance department	Lack of financial skills
Access to short/long term capital	Tight finances
Good relationship with suppliers	Poor relationship with suppliers
Efficient cost control system	Ineffective cost control system
Healthy sales position	Weak or volatile sales
Flexibile budgeting and pricing	Inflexible budgeting and pricing
Effective use of accounting technology	Dated accounting system

Problems/Issue Identification Matrix — The External Environment

Operations

Opportunities	**Threats**
Cost reduction due to new technology	Higher cost of technology
Reduction in competition	Increased competition
Favourable change in consumer law	Unfavourable change in consumer law

Marketing

Opportunities	**Threats**
Recognition of changing consumer demand	Ignorance of changing consumer demand
Influx of new consumers to the market	Shrinking consumer market
Changing leisure habits in new markets	Leisure habits moving away from hospitality focus
Potential growth of market in Eastern Europe and developing countries	Stagnation of expansion in foreign markets

	Opportunities	**Threats**

Personnel

	Expansion of sources of labour	Shrinking labour market
	Changes in educational system producing better qualified employees	Poorly qualified recruits
	Better training facilities	Poorer training facilities

Finance

	Lower interest rates	Increased interest rates
	Availability of venture capital	Difficulty in borrowing
	Use of alternative suppliers	Supplier monopoly
	Availability of grant aid or EC finance	Lack of grant support
	Higher discretionary income of consumers	Lower discretionary income of consumers

This matrix is by no means exhaustive. It provides a check list of the type of issue that will emerge from researching a case study. It is important to summarise information in each of the four categories, bearing in mind there may be grey areas between the internal and external environments. From the matrix, you should have gathered sufficient information to undertake the decision making stage of the case study answer.

Formulating and Evaluating Alternative Solutions

There is no correct course of action for any of the cases in this book. Each will have a number of possible solutions and it is part of the learning process that you should evaluate all possible alternatives and select the one which you consider to be the most appropriate. There are often numerous solutions to a situation and the task is to select the one which is most likely to produce, or come closest to, the desired result.

Selection of the most appropriate solution must be undertaken in a systematic fashion or else a clearly defined problem may be tackled inappropriately. There are numerous well-documented, decision-making techniques available but a simple method is suggested here:

1. Write down a range of possibilities, listing the advantages and disadvantages of each.

2. Delete all those courses of action that are not applicable because of operational constraints. These constraints could include: insufficient capital available for major renovation; limitations due to licencing laws; staff skills not sufficient for a more complex menu; an unattractive location for certain customers.

3. When all the constraints have been examined fully, the range of options will be considerably narrower. The most promising alternatives — possibly two ot three — should then be examined to identify the likely outcomes of each. While complex decision tree analysis requires considerable statistical calculation, a simplified approach can assist in the broader evaluation of each outcome. For

example, a restauranteur with poor trading results may wish to trade-up with a more complex menu, or trade-down with a simplified menu, or close that operation and move to a better location, and so on.

Taking the first two options only, you should attempt to estimate the sales likely from each course of action. If, in this example, the restaurant is located in a town with no other quality restaurant but several branded fast-food chains, then it may be reasonable to suggest that the restauranteur trade-up to avoid competition and to dominate the quality eating out market. In the face of limited information, this would seem to offer a more likely solution to the problem than trading-down. If further information in the example pointed out that a significant proportion of residents in the town had high discretionary incomes, then this may add to the suggestion to trade-up. This process should continue until a reasonable case can be drawn for the most appropriate alternative.

Each case study will provide certain information that will allow reasonable conclusions to be drawn. This is certainly not an exact approach, but it will provide a reasonable indication of the relative merits of alternative courses of action. Once the short list of alternatives has been narrowed down to one, the implementation stage of the decision making process can be undertaken.

Implementation of a Chosen Course of Action
Making a decision is one thing, putting a decision into practice can be another. The time restraints and logistics of implementation may cause managers to re-evaluate the worth of the course of action selected. If the evaluation stage has been properly undertaken, then modifications are usually only minor in nature. However, if the selected course of action has not been fully planned, this will become apparent when the implementation or action plan stage of the case study report is written.

2 Financial analysis

The financial aspects of the case studies in this book have been emphasised, because profitability is normally the central objective to any commercial business. Similarly, many business issues which appear to be nonfinancial, once fully analysed, have important financial implications which would be foolish to ignore. This section will outline important aspects of operations finance that will be useful in case study preparation.

Financial analysis

Despite the apparent complexity which surround the financial aspects of cases, the issues or problems involved can usually be located in a handful of categories such as those outlined in Problem/Issue Identification Matrix (see page 7). The relevant information can be dispersed within the text of the case — in the form of average spend figures, room rates or menu prices, for example — or, alternatively, in more detailed financial statements or reports. These are usually in the form of:

- The trading and profit and loss account

- The cash flow forecast

- The balance sheet.

From an operational perspective, the trading and profit and loss account and the cash flow statement are the most important. The trading and profit and loss account summarises the past period's sales, expenses and profitability, while the cash flow statement shows the all-important flow of cash to and from the business. The balance sheet is a snapshot of the overall financial position of the business at a particular moment in time and includes the value of assets, the extent of business liabilities, the extent of working capital and a summary of shareholders' capital.

Ratio analysis

Financial information can be analysed in numerous ways but ratio analysis is a technique by which data are given a mathematical expression in order that a significant relationship can be shown with other data. Analysis of the trading and profit and loss account of a single company for one year will provide some useful information. However, this information can be made to reveal much more about the relative performance of that business if there are benchmarks with which to compare the figures. There are several common methods by which one set of data can be compared with other information. Three common methods are:

1. *Cross sectional analysis*: performance measured against that of other similar companies or industrial norms.

2. *Time series analysis:* performance of one company measured over a number of years.

3. *Variance analysis:* performance of one company measured against budget.

Once benchmarks are established, ratio analysis can be used to simplify examination of all three methods. The ratios are usually divided into groups, each with different emphasis. Approaches differ, but some of the more commonly applicable ratios are grouped as follows:

Liquidity Ratios

Liquidity ratios measure the operation's ability to meet its short-term liabilities with assets readily available.

Current ratio $\dfrac{\text{Current assets}}{\text{Current liabilities}}$

The current ratio measures the liquidity of the firm by analysis of the relationship between current assets and current liabilities. The excess of assets over liabilities is called working capital. Generally, hospitality businesses require less working capital than manufacturing firms.

Acid Test/Quick ratio $\dfrac{\text{Quick assets}}{\text{Current liabilities}}$

Quick assets are assets easily convertible into cash. Current assets less inventories are quick assets. This is a more stringent test of liquidity than the current ratio, as some inventory items may take some months to convert into cash.

Debtor's period ratio $\dfrac{\text{Debtors}}{\text{Credit sales}} \times 365$

The debtor's period ratio measures the average time it takes (in days, weeks or months) to collect debts from credit customers. The more quickly a firm can collect outstanding accounts from clients, the more liquid will be the firm's position. Long debtor's periods may indicate bad credit control practices, but too short a period may mean some clients who require certain credit facilities will consider using other operators. A debtor's collection period of approximately 30 days appears to be common in the hotel sector.

Creditor's peroid ratio $\dfrac{\text{Creditors}}{\text{Credit purchases}} \times 365$

Similar to the debtor's period ratio, the creditor's period ratio indicates how long it takes for credit purchases to be paid. A creditor's collection period of approximately 30 days appears to be common in the hotel sector.

Gearing Ratios

If the firm is financed in part by debentures or preference shares (fixed interest capital), then it must cover interest payments each year — even during periods of low profitability. It is important for the firm to have the right balance between fixed interest capital and total capital employed.

Gearing ratio $\dfrac{\text{Long-term fixed interest capital}}{\text{Total long-term capital employed}}$

A highly-geared company is one with a significant proportion of total capital in the form of fixed interest capital. Under certain circumstances, that business will be more vulnerable to insolvency than a company with lower gearing.

Profitability Ratios

These ratios show how effective the firm has been in using its resources to produce profit. The higher the ratio, the greater the level of profitability.

$$\text{Return on capital employed ratio} \quad \frac{\text{Net profit}}{\text{Capital employed}}$$

The return on capital employed is one ratio that compares operational profit (usually before tax) with balance sheet items, in this case capital employed. Such ratios are useful in that they provide a general indication of how profitable investment in certain sectors can be (if we use an *average* company for each comparison). The net profit figure (either before or after tax) is shown as a ratio of capital employed (usually total assets less current liabilities). In essence, this ratio provides an indication of how effectively the assets of the firm have been used to produce profit.

$$\text{Gross profit ratio} \quad \frac{\text{Sales} - \text{Cost of sales}}{\text{Sales}}$$

This is the primary internal calculation for food and beverage departments. A general rule of thumb for the industry is 65 per cent gross profit for food and beverage outlets, but variations occur depending on the type of operation.

$$\text{Departmental Profit ratio} \quad \frac{\text{Sales} - \text{Direct expenses}}{\text{Sales}}$$

Each department can be analysed after direct costs have been deducted to compare profitability. The importance of departmental analysis is that problems can be pinpointed and solved accordingly. Generally, the expenses here are controllable and therefore should receive as much attention as is cost effective from the manager.

$$\text{Net profit ratio:} \quad \frac{\text{Net profit}}{\text{Sales}}$$

Activity Ratios

These are used in close connection with profitability ratios and provide operational information about revenue and expenses in relation to budgets, competitors or industry averages.

$$\text{Average room rate ratio} \quad \frac{\text{Room revenue}}{\text{Rooms sold}}$$

$$\text{Room occupancy ratio} \quad \frac{\text{Rooms occupied}}{\text{Rooms available}}$$

$$\text{Guests per room ratio} \quad \frac{\text{Numer of guests}}{\text{Rooms occupied}}$$

$$\text{Average spend ratio (food or beverage)} \quad \frac{\text{Sales}}{\text{Number of guests}}$$

$$\text{Restaurant turnover ratio} \quad \frac{\text{Number of guests}}{\text{Number of seats}}$$

$$\text{Average waiter sales ratio} \quad \frac{\text{Sales}}{\text{Number of waiters}}$$

$$\text{Cost of sales percentage ratio} \quad \frac{\text{Cost of sales}}{\text{Sales}}$$

$$\text{Labour cost percentage ratio} \quad \frac{\text{Labour cost}}{\text{Sales}}$$

A worked example: Vintage Hotels and Branded Inns

A worked example will demonstrate the type of analysis that will be required for the case studies. A cross-sectional analysis is demonstrated with a selection of the possible ratios. Vintage Hotels and Branded Inns are two groups operating in the hotel sector. Below are balance sheets and trading and profit and loss accounts for the year to January 1990.

SUMMARISED BALANCE SHEET AS AT 1 JAN 1990 £(000)

	Vintage Hotels £		Branded Inns £	
Fixed assets				
Land and buildings		265		515
Plant and equipment		8		26
		273		541
Current assets				
Stock	92		51	
Debtors	38		38	
Cash at bank	13		30	
	143		119	
Current liabilities				
Creditors	89		49	
Overdraft	39	15	64	6
	128	288	113	547
Long term liabilities				
Debentures		170		220
		118		327
Shareholders equity				
Ordinary share capital		94		282
Retained profit		24		45
		118		327

SUMMARISED TRADING AND PROFIT AND LOSS ACCOUNTS AS AT JANUARY 1990.

Vintage Hotels

	Sales £	Cost of sales £	Dept labour £	Dept expenses £	Dept profit £
Rooms	400	–	102	36	262
Food	332	129	66	29	108
Beverage	108	44	30	4	30
					400
Undistributed operating expenses					210
Fixed charges					85
Net profit					105

Branded Inns

	Sales £	Cost of sales £	Dept labour £	Dept expenses £	Dept profit £
Rooms	1,200	–	273	91	836
Food	615	216	178	61	160
Beverage	375	116	68	27	164
					1,160
Undistributed operating expenses					638
Fixed charges					203
Net profit					319

Additional information:

60% of Vintage Hotels sales are credit; 40% are cash
20% of Branded Inns sales are credit; 80% are cash
40% of Vintage Inns purchases are credit; 10% are cash
90% of Branded Inns purchases are credit; 10% are cash.

By expressing balance sheet and trading and profit and loss account figures as ratios, it is possible to get a clearer financial picture of each company before we employ more complex ratios.

EXPRESSING BALANCE SHEET INFORMATION AS RATIOS (PER CENT ROUNDED)

	Vintage Hotels %	Branded Inns %
Assets		
Land and buildings	64	78
Plant and equipment	2	4
Stock	22	8
Debtors	9	6
Cash at bank	3	4
	100	100
Liabilities and shareholder's equity		
Creditors	21	7
Overdraft	9	10
Debentures	41	33
Ordinary share capital	23	43
Retained profit	6	7
	100	100

EXPRESSED TRADING AND PROFIT AND LOSS ACCOUNT INFORMATION AS RATIOS (PER CENT ROUNDED)

Vintage Hotels

	Sales %	Cost of sales %	Dept labour %	Dept expenses %	Dept profit %
Rooms	48	0	26	9	65
Food	39	39	20	9	32
Beverage	13	41	28	3	28
Operating income					48
Undistributed operating expenses					25
Fixed charges					10
Net profit					13

Branded Hotels

	Sales %	Cost of sales %	Dept labour %	Dept expenses %	Dept profit %
Rooms	55	0	23	8	69
Food	28	35	29	10	26
Beverage	17	31	18	7	44
Operating income					53
Undistributed operating expenses					29
Fixed charges					9
Net profit					15

(Departmental percentages within the boxes are ratios of departmental sales. All other percentages are ratios of total sales.)

From the balance sheets we can make some initial observations. Both Branded Inns and Vintage Hotels have a high proportion of fixed assets. This reflects the fact that property consitutes a significant proportion of the assets of any hotel company. Vintage Hotels have considerably higher levels of stock than Branded Inns. Unless there was a significant difference in operation, one would question why so much stock is being held and cost not put to better use. A higher proportion of Vintage Inns' current liabilities are creditors, again this may have implications for the business if creditors' demand to be paid and current assets are insufficient to cover such demands. Further observations of this type can be made, but a more detailed investigation can be undertaken by the use of the ratios introduced above on both balance sheets and trading and profit and loss accounts.

Liquidity Ratios
Current ratio

Vintage Hotels	Branded Inns
$\frac{143}{128} = 1.12$	$\frac{119}{113} = 1.05$

Both companies are able to cover current liabilities out of current assets. However, a point of caution is that too high a current ratio could mean too much stock is being carried or that the number of debtors is excessive.

Acid test

Vintage Hotels	Branded Inns
$\frac{143 - 92}{128} = 0.4$	$\frac{119 - 51}{113} = 0.6$

This shows a slightly different situation. Vintage Hotels can cover only 40 per cent of its current liabilities out of quick assets. It may be in the interest of this company to reduce its stock holding and increase its cash reserves.

Debtor's period ratio

Vintage Hotels	Branded Inns
$\frac{38}{504} \times 365 = 28$ days	$\frac{38}{440} \times 365 = 32$ days

Creditor's period ratio

Vintage Hotels	Branded Inns
$\frac{89}{156} \times 365 = 208$ days	$\frac{49}{299} \times 365 = 60$ days

From this we can see that Vintage Hotels takes over six months to pay its creditors. This may be seen as a benefit to it as cash remains within the business for as long as possible. However, some creditors may offer discounts for early payment or penalties for late payment. Similarly, some suppliers may eventually refuse to trade with bad payers.

Gearing ratio

Vintage Hotels	Branded Inns
$\frac{170}{288} = 0.59$	$\frac{220}{547} = 0.40$

Both companies appear not to be over-burdened with long-term debt, with Branded Inns being in a slightly stronger position. From the creditors' point of view, this ratio is important because they need to know that they will be able to recover a loan in the event of bankruptcy.

Profitability Ratios

Return on capital employed

<table>
<tr><td>Vintage Hotels</td><td>Branded Inns</td></tr>
<tr><td>$\frac{105}{288} = 36.5$</td><td>$\frac{319}{547} = 58.3$</td></tr>
</table>

Both companied have high returns although Branded Inns are making considerably better use of capital employed than Vintage Hotels.

Gross profit ratio (food and beverage)

<table>
<tr><td>Vintage Hotels</td><td>Branded Inns</td></tr>
<tr><td>$\frac{267}{440} = 60.6\%$</td><td>$\frac{658}{970} = 66.4\%$</td></tr>
</table>

Vintage Hotels achieved modest gross profit levels. This could be because of sales mix bias towards low gross profit sales, incorrect pricing or a variety of internal control problems. Separate gross profit ratios for food and for beverage would also be calculated for both groups.

Net profit ratio

<table>
<tr><td>Vintage Hotels</td><td>Branded Inns</td></tr>
<tr><td>$\frac{105}{840} = 12.5$</td><td>$\frac{319}{2190} = 14.5$</td></tr>
</table>

Branded Inns has a healthy profit margin while Vintage Hotels could improve although its profit margin is still reasonable. Both could achieve a higher net profit if gross profit problems were resolved.

Current statistical data

Published sources of statistics can be of considerable use when working on a case study. These can be used together with internal historical information and intercompany comparisons to provide information for the accurate assessment of case material and for budget preparation in responses. Some useful statistics are as follows:

Operational information (UK)

Sales mix (departments as a percentage of total sales revenue)

Rooms	47.7%
Food	31.0%
Beverage	14.7%
Minor depts	3.6%
Rental and other income	3.0%

Amount per cover — food sales (average spend by department)

Restaurant	£8.23
Room service	£4.76
Banqueting	£9.97

Distribution of expenses (as a percentage of total sales revenue)

Food cost	11.0%
Beverage cost	5.0%
Payroll and related expences	27.3%
Department expenses	11.0%
Administrative and general	4.6%
Energy cost	2.9%
Property operation and maintenance	2.2%
Marketing	2.0%
Gross operating profit	34.0%

Cost of sales (as a percentage of departmental sales revenue)

Food	34.4%
Beverage	35.3%

Departmental operating profit (as a persentage of departmental sales revenue)

Rooms	76.1%
Food and beverage	38.0%

Market information

Average annual room occupancy

UK	68.1%
London	76.2%
Provinces	66.0%
Scotland	66.7%

Average number of guests per room

UK	1.52
London	1.42
Provinces	1.71
Scotland	1.44

Average daily room rate

UK	£47.51
London	£74.90
Provinces	£40.78
Scotland	£39.02

Average rate per guest night

UK	£43.84
London	£59.60
Provinces	£26.02
Scotland	£39.82

Guest analysis — origin of guests

UK	57.0%
Other Europe	13.9%
USA and Canada	17.1%
Central & South America	0.9%
Japan	3.4%
Other Asia	2.4%
Middle East	2.4%
Australasia	1.5%
North Africa	0.4%
Other Africa	1.0%

Guest analysis — type of guest

Business travellers	39.3%
Holiday tourist	28.3%
Conference delegates	13.0%
Government officials	1.7%
Other	17.1%

Guest analysis — reservations

Guests with advanced reservations	92.5%
Repeat guests	41.6%

Guest analysis — payment of account

Cash	23.2%
Credit card	39.2%
Other credit	37.6%

Source: Horwath Consulting (1990), *United Kingdom Hotel Industry*

Key ratios

	Hotels	Restaurants	Breweries	Retail*
Return on assets	3.7	8.1	7.6	11.0
Return on capital	4.6	14.0	9.5	18.4
Profit margin pre tax	14.7	5.0	13.1	6.6
Current ratio	0.4	0.5	0.8	0.8
Quick ratio	0.4	0.4	0.5	0.5

* Retailers are included here in order to provide comparison with another consumer sector.

Source: ICC Information Group Ltd (1990), *Industrial Performance Analysis*

3 Writing your report

Introduction

The majority of case studies will require a response in the form of a management report — an essay or similar narrative style is less appropriate. The following notes are intended for guidance in preparation of report-style responses.

A report is a document which methodically and objectively presents information accurately and concisely to a specific reader. Of varying length, but with an emphasis on brevity, it usually falls into one of three categories according to the terms of reference given in the case study:

Analytical/explanatory. To present an objective interpretation of facts with views/ options given if requested. This should interpret historical information and evidence and explain it with clarity and simplicity.

Response led/creative. To present a solution or a set of solutions to a given individual or a set of individuals.

Persuasive. To present a response which is aimed at approval or agreement from the reader. Thus any recommended course of action should be directly marketed to the reader.

Your client

In writing the report it is necessary to take into account your client/reader's needs, attitudes, and knowledge of the topic of your report. These considerations will influence your choice of content as well as the kind of language used. Ask yourself these questions:

- Who is the client/reader?

- Why does he or she want the report?

- What kind of language will he or she understand?

- What does he or she already know about the topic?

There are four stages to consider in the production of a report:

1. Preparation

2. Organization

3. Writing

4. Revision.

Preparation

Good preparation is the basis of an effective report. Initially, it is important to establish clearly the topic and purpose of the report. Then to establish the terms of reference or specific instructions. Finally, to keep your reader/client firmly in mind as data or information is collected for the report.

The case study will contain certain information, but you may need to gather information about the external environment which does not come directly from the case. Such information will provide you with a more realistic scenario for the case study. Before collecting any data, review the case study's purpose and attempt to anticipate likely difficulties that may be encountered. Start by checking material already available within the business, then move to reference works, periodicals, statistical surveys, consultants' reports and other publications. Only after these secondary sources have been examined should original research be undertaken.

Study the information collected, and evaluate it according to the standards of the topic and to the terms of reference of the report. Not all facts, statements or ideas, even from within the case itself, will be of equal relevance, nor will all be objectively written. Verify facts, test statements, and weigh ideas for their soundness in the process of sifting through the material. In particular, beware of subjective opinions given in the case study — they may be of little use. After the initial sifting, retain only that information which is sound and relevant to the report.

Organisation
Careful organisation of the material is essential for effective use of time and the systematic production of the finished report. There are several ways in which this can be done, all of which should provide an adequate result. However, bear in mind that it is important to adopt a system of numbering and lettering within the report that provides a logical and easy-to-read text.

Numbering and Lettering
In using numbers and letters for the main headings, subheadings and paragraphs of the report, it is necessary to be aware of the insitutional practices and the client's/reader's requirements. The following examples are commonly used in a variety of combinations:

- Letters (upper or lower case)
- Numbers
- Roman numerals (I, II, III, etc)
- Modified decimal system :1.1, 1.2, 1.3; 2.1, 2.2, 2.3, etc).

The report should be numbered in consecutive order starting with the summary or abstract page, with the numbers in the upper right-hand corner of each page. Appendix pages should also be numbered or lettered.

Statistics
The use of statistics and/or visuals in the report can enhance its content and presentation. The following are offered as suggestions for guidance:

- Figures and illustrations in the text should be used only where appropriate.
- Visuals should be neatly mounted and bordered.
- Explain any symbols used.
- Explain the significance of any statistics used.

- Assign each visual a figure number and identifying caption.

Appendicies

The appendicies will consist of calculations, statistics, large diagrams, and other supplementary material. If there are a number of appendicies, they should be identified (1, 2, 3, for example) in consecutive order and placed as the final section of your report. In the text, reference should be made to the relevant appendix in order to give the reader the opportunity to examine a particular item of data more closely.

Writing

It is advised that the report is written in at least two drafts. The first draft will be rough, requiring correction and rewriting. The second, corrected draft will be prepared in fair copy, preferably typed. Prior to preparation of the second draft, you should reread it objectively and critically, as if it were someone else's work.

The use of language

Here are some points to consider about language in the report:

- Keep sentences short.

- Use familiar and specific words in preference to abstract ones.

- Be sparing in the use of adverbs and adjectives.

- Avoid jargon and slang.

- Explain terms the reader may not understand in footnotes, or in a glossary of terms.

- Avoid personalising statements.

The presentation and appearance of the report should, where possible, reveal its structure. Page after page of unbroken text without the help of headings and subheadings will be difficult to interpret and will not fulfil the objectives of the exercise. The following approach is one that can be easily adopted:

Title page

The title page should contain all the information that any reader would need to know if he or she were to refer to your report as a source in a bibliography. It should include:

- The name of the organisation which prepared the report.

- The name of the organisation for which the report is written.

- The title of the report, which briefly states the topic.

- The name of the author.

- The date of the report.

Contents page

To aid the reader, a contents page should be inserted immediately after the title page. The contents page should consist of a list of all the items in the report, such as the headings, subheadings, figures, bibliography, and appendices. These items should be placed down the left-hand side of the page. Begin numbering the pages with the first 'item' in the report — the executive summary or abstract.

Executive summary/abstract
To assist the reader gain a general view of the contents of the report, and to save the reader time, a short summary or abstract of the topic is placed just after the contents page and before the introduction. The summary or abstract may also include keywords. The length of this section should be no more than 150 to 200 words.

Introduction
This important section of your report should also be brief (150 to 200 words). The introduction should state the purpose of the report, name the main subject areas and give an indication of your conclusion. The introduction may also be used to define a situation, theme, or subject, and indicate the extent and significance of the report. The introduction constitutes the outline of the whole report.

Analysis
The analysis section is the subject matter of your report in which particular aspects are developed in a logical and coherent manner. These are presented under a number of appropriate subheadings identifying the subdivisions of the analysis.

Recommendations
The recommendations of the report stem directly from the facts, statements and ideas presented in the analysis. They should be of an advisory nature and should clearly indicate the action requested. Tabulation of information is sometimes helpful in the presentation of recommendations. Practical implementation is of key importance when deciding upon the recommendations, which should be brief and easily understandable.

Action plan
Increasingly, consultants are using the 'Action plan' as a subsection of 'Recommendations'. The action plan provides a prioritised summary and timetable of the implementation of management directed change to improve the current situation as disclosed via the analysis. The action plan is an essential selling medium of many consultant's reports. It provides an obvious and immediate guide to practical implementation of solutions to operational management problems.

Revision
Before preparing the final copy of the report, consider the following points:

- Look at the draft as a whole. Is the design clear? Are the headings consistent with their purpose?

- Examine all the pages in relation to one another. Are they consistent with one another? Have you stated the purpose of your report and main subject areas, etc. clearly in the introduction?

- Consider each statement in the text for accuracy and coherence.

- Retain only those facts, reliable statements, and ideas which are relevant to the topic.

- Make sure that you have not omitted any facts, assumptions or propositions necessary to forming the logical conclusion to your report.

- Have you provided referenced support for your arguments?

4 How to quote references

When producing a case study response, it is essential to quote your sources of reference, and to acknowledge the books and periodicals used. The reasons for this are twofold: it affords evidence of research and provides justification for your responses, and the reader is able to follow up and continue your work by going back to the original sources. There are a variety of ways of quoting references. One simple method, The Harvard System, will be demonstrated. Using this method, work is quoted by citing the author's surname and date of publication in the text of the response:

Either
It has been suggested that technical management must be recognised as part of a larger management system (Douglas & Jones, 1989)

Or
Atkinson (1986) suggests catering performs a different role for consumers than for producers.

Points for guidance
1. Page numbers should be included where there is a need to be specific. For example:
   East (1980:p38) suggests that a simple model of management is ". . . the study of control, coordination and organisation".

2. When quoting more than one document published by an author in the same year, distinguished between them by adding lower case letters (a, b, c, etc) after the year of publication.

3. If there are two authors, the surnames of both should be given. For example:
   For many goods, the caterer cannot rely on previous purchases since by the time repurchase occurs, product development presents a different choice situation (Simkins and Peters, 1988).

4. If there are more than two authors, the surname of the first author may be given, followed by '*et al*' (which means 'and others'). For example:
   The choice of catering products is frequently based on personal values (Peters *et al*, 1978).

5. If there is no apparent author use Anon (for anonymous) and the date.

How to present a full reference

When you quote the full reference at the end of the report using the Harvard system, the following elements should be included.

Books or Separately Issued Publications
Author, Editor etc
Year of Publication (the copyright data, that is, the date of that edition)

Title (italicised when printed, but underlined when typed)
Edition (If not the first edition)
Publisher (can be abbreviated by leaving out initials).
When all the elements are put together, a reference may be like the following example:

Makinson, Kenneth (1978): *Food, Catering and Health* (2nd edition), Hodder and Stoughton.

Points for guidance

1. If there are more than two authors, quote the first followed by *et al*. For example:
Smith, John R. *et al* (1978): *The Consumer: The Art of Buying*, Prentice Hall.

2. List an edited work under the name of the editor. For example:
Smith, D. A. and Dyson, S. (Eds) (1978): *Catering and Health: A Search for the Consumer Interest* (3rd edition), The Free Press.

3. If the work has been produced by an organisation, committee, etc. treat the name of the organisation as the author. For example:
Department of Employment (1982): *Family Expenditure Survey 1980*, HMSO.

4. If you are quoting a chapter or a portion of a publication the following may be used:
Hoel, Paul (1971): *Elementary Statistics* (2nd edition), Wiley, Ch 8.

Periodicals and Journals

Author(s) of article
Title of article
Name of periodical (italicised when printed, but underlined when typed)
Volume (italicised when printed, but underlined when typed); Part (in brackets), for example, *6*(3) or Vol. 6 (No. 3).
Pages
Date of issue (including week or month where relevant).
Put together, a reference will be like the following example:

Nichols, Alison: Hotel and catering — The Missing Link With Consumers? *Journal of Catering Studies*: 5(2), pp. 237–240, June 1989.

5 Bibliography

This bibliography is divided into two parts:

- General references in major subject areas and

- Recent specific references.

Neither part is by any means exhaustive but each part represents the authors' suggestions for background reading.

General References

Finance

Coltman, M. M. (1987): *Hospitality Management Accounting* (3rd edition), Van Nostrand Reinhold.

Harris, P. and Hazzard, P. (1987): *Managerial Accounting in the Hotel and Catering Industry*, Hutchinson.

Horwath Consulting (1990): *United Kingdom Hotel Industry 1990,* Horwath Consulting.

ICC Information Group Ltd. (1990): *Business Ratio Report*, ICC Information Group Ltd.

ICC Information Group Ltd. (1990): *Keynote Report: Hotels*, ICC Information Group Ltd.

ICC Information Group Ltd. (1990): *Keynote Report: Restaurants,* ICC Information Group Ltd.

ICC Information Group Ltd. (1990): *Industrial Performance Analysis*, ICC Information Group Ltd.

Kotas, R. (1987): *Management Accounting for Hotels and Restaurants*, Surrey University Press.

Marketing

Baker, M. J., (1985): *Marketing: an Introductory Text* (4th edition), Macmillan.

Buttle, F. (1986): *Hotel and Foodservice Marketing*, Holt, Rienhart and Winston.

Courtis, J., (1987): *Marketing Services — A Practical Guide*, Kogan Page.

Cowell, D. (1984): *The Marketing of Services*, Heinemann.

Green, M. (1987): *Marketing Hotels and Restaurants into the 90's* (2nd edition), Heinemann.

Operations and General

Braham, B. (1985): *Hotel Front Office*, Hutchinson.

Davis, B. and Stone, S. (1987): *Food and Beverage Management*, Heinemann.

Littlejohn, D. (ed) (1988): *Britain's Catering Industry*, Jordans.

Miller, J. E. (1987): *Menu Pricing and Strategy*, Van Nostrand Reinhold.

Rutes, W. A. and Penner, R. H. (1985): *Hotel Planning and Design,* Architectual Press.

Personnel

Boella, M. J. (1983): *Personnel Management in the Hotel and Catering Industry* (3rd edition), Hutchinson.

Cowling, A. G., and Mailer, C. J. B. (1981): *Managing Human Resources*, Edward Arnold.

Magurn, J. P. (1983): *A Manual of Staff Management in the Hotel and Catering Industry*, Heinemann.

Mars, G., Bryant, D., and Mitchell, P. (1979); *Manpower Problems in the Hotel and Catering Industry*, Gower.

Recent specific references

Budget Hotels/Motels

Bond, C.: Budget Beds Will Meet All Needs. *Hospitality:* p. 8, June 1988.

Coulton, A.: Red Roof Inns: Beyond 'Sleep Cheap'. *Lodging Hospitality:* pp. 27–30, September 1989.

Dane, J: Budget Breakthrough. *London Restaurant Business*: pp. 16–17, 25 January 1988.

Gilbert, D. and Arnold, L.: Budget Hotels II. *Leisure Management:* pp. 70–1, 81, April 1989.

McWhirter, A.: No Frills, Low Bills. *Business Traveller:* pp. 11–14, October 1989.

Rowe, M.: Budget Lodging: Poised for the '90s. *Lodging Hospitality:* pp. 45–6, 48, September 1989.

Somerville, J.: UK, France Lead Europe's Economy Hotel Expansion, *Hotel and Restaurants International*: pp. 50–2, 54, February 1988.

Walsh-Herron, J.: Motels No Longer at the Crossroads. *Leisure Management:* pp. 73–4, March 1988.

Conference and Banqueting

Chester. C.: In pursuit of Excellence. *Meetings and Incentive Travel:* pp. 58–62, April 1988.

Gordon, R., Sparrow, S. and Wood, A.: Conferences Buckle Down. *Caterer and Hotelkeeper:* pp. 54–6, 59, 5 October 1989.

Hamilton, A.: Seats of Learning. *Conference Britain:* pp. 31, 33, 34, September/October 1989.

Harmer, J.: Running a Wedding. *Caterer and Hotelkeeper:* pp. 32–4, 25 August 1988.

Longbottom, P.: No Longer Purely Academic. *Meetings and Incentive Travel:* pp. 35–42, July/August 1989.

Martins, C.: Pipe Dreams Come True. *Conference Britain*: pp. 15–17, July/August 1989.

Plume, R.: M25 Venus: Motorway Meetings, *Conference and Exhibitions:* pp. 303–33, July/August 1989.

Tyler, G.: Catering for the Business Customer. *Catering:* pp. 71–5, October 1989.

Ward, P.: Conferences — How Talk Shows Profit. *Caterer and Hotelkeeper:* pp. 40–5, 25 August 1988.

Weston, S.: Join the Meet Industry. *Catering and Accommodation Management:* pp. 8–9, August 1989.

Wood, H.: Back to College. *Travel GBI:* pp. 22–24, November 1989.

Contract Catering

Tyler, G.: Civil Service. *Caterer and Hotelkeeper:* pp. 72–4, 12 October 1989.

Wyatt, C.: Campus Cuisine. *Caterer and Hotelkeeper:* pp. 58–9, 26 October 1989.

Fast Food

Gardner, N.: Delivering Growth Fast. *Caterer and Hotelkeeper:* pp. 126–7, 130, 3 November 1988.

Pettipher, L.: Blazing Griddles. *Caterer and Hotelkeeper:* pp. 46–7, 26 October 1989.

Thompson, J.: Fast Food, the Continuing Success. *Hospitality:* pp. 10, 12, 16–17, November 1988.

Trollope, K.: Room for Improvement. *Restauranteur:* pp. 25–6, December/January 1989.

Ward, P.: Dial a Dinner. *Caterer and Hotelkeeper*: pp. 34–6, 4 August 1988.

Waters, P.: Price Check on the High Street Chains. *Popular Foodservice:* pp. 28, 30, 33, July/August 1988.

Finance

Carr, D.: Turning Hotel Restaurants into Profit Centres. *Cornell Hotel and Restaurant Administration Quarterly:* pp. 15, 16, February 1988.

Cole, N.: Staying Power. *Caterer and Hotelkeeper.* pp. 60–1, 4 May 1989.

Gordon, R.: Money Talk. *Caterer and Hotelkeeper.* Supplement. p. 7, 25 May 1989.

Goymour, D.: Tariff Survey: Gently Does It. *Caterer and Hotelkeeper:* pp. 46–8, 50, 8 June 1989.

Relihan, W. J.: The Yield Management Approach to Hotel-Room Pricing, *Cornell Hotel and Restaurant Administration Quarterly.* pp. 40–5, May 1989.

Schmidgall, R. S. and Ninemeier, J.: Budgeting Practice in Lodging and Food Service Chains: An Analysis and Comparisons. *Hospitality Management*: Vol. 8 (No. 1) pp. 35–41, 1989.

Taylor, D.: Peripheral Vision. *Caterer and Hotelkeeper:* pp. 39–40, 9 November 1989.

Ward, P.: How to Write a Business Plan. *Caterer and Hotelkeeper:* pp. 40, 43, 46, 16 June 1988.

General Trends

Barrett, F.: A Night in the Country. *Management Today:* pp. 105, 108, 110, April 1988.

Catering: The Bottom Line of the Leisure Industry. Leisure Week: pp. 15–18, 1 December 1989.

Chester, C.: Hotel Bookings: Via Central Office or Direct? *Meetings and Incentive Travel:* pp. 26–33, September 1989.

Clough, J.: Health Clubs '87. *Leisure Management:* pp. 39–42, January 1988.

Daniele, D. W.: All-Suite Players Project Major Growth. *Hotel and Motel Management:* pp. 52, 54, 56, 30 May 1988.

Harwood, G., and Frankis, E.: Country Club Hotels. *Leisure Management:* pp. 29, 30, November 1989.

Jones, E.: The Waiting Game. *Caterer and Hotelkeeper:* pp. 46–7, 49, 1 December 1988.

Legate, P.: Recycling the Ancestral Home. *Hospitality:* 16–19, September 1988.

Ward, P.: Waltham Abbey Nest. *Caterer and Hotelkeeper:* pp. 74–5, 77, 1 September 1988.

Ward, P.: Country Clubs Get in the Swing. *Caterer and Hotelkeeper:* pp. 34–6, 10 March 1988.

Kitchen/Restaurant Design and Fittings
Caterer and Hotelkeeper: The Show Must Go On. *Caterer and Housekeeper:* pp. 64–6, 12 October 1989.
Harmer, J.: Restaurant Planning. *Caterer and Hotelkeeper.* pp. 54–7, 13 October 1988.
Homer, S.: Glass Class. *Caterer and Hotelkeeper:* pp. 147–150, 2 November 1989.
Homer, S.: Topping Out. *Caterer and Hotelkeeper:* pp. 91–8, 9 November 1989.
Hope, S.: Preparing a Design Brief. *British Hotelier and Restauranteur:* pp. 22–3, 25, 27, September 1989.
Lewis, A.: Cook-Chill Catering. *Food Science and Technology Today:* pp. 214–17, September 1988.
Rozario, K.: Kitchen Design. *Pub Caterer:* p. 38, October 1988.
Ryle, M.: Design and Decor. *Pub Caterer:* pp. 53–6, October 1989.
Ryle, M.: A Kitchen Re-Think. *Pub Caterer:* pp. 21–4, May 1989.
Symington, M.: Cook Chill Good or Bad? *Catering*: pp. 47, 50, 52, April 1989.
Whitehall, B.: Cold Encounter. *Caterer and Hotelkeeper:* pp. 94–6, 6 July 1989.

Marketing
Backman, P. and Fieldhouse, M.: Bringing Seafood to the Customer. *Seafood International:* pp. 30, 32, August 1988.
Bond, C.: Hotels Get Advertising into Focus. *Hospitality:* p. 6, February 1988.
Caterer and Hotelkeeper Supplement: Read all about it. *Caterer and Hotelkeeper:* pp. 8–9, September 1986.
Chester, C.: Hotel Bookings Via Central Office or Direct? *Meetings and Incentive Travel.* pp. 26–33, September 1989.
Drinkwater, C.: Leisure Marketing in Action. *Leisure Management:* pp. 49, 50, December 1987.
Feltenstein, T.: Restaurant Franchising: Is There Still Room for Survival? *Cornell Hotel and Restaurant Administration Quarterly:* pp. 8–11, May 1988.
Green, M: 131 Ways to Double Your Profits. *Caterer and Hotelkeeper:* Various issues through November and December 1989.
Martin, W.: Moving Targets. *Leisure Management*: pp. 26–9, June 1988.
Wall, M.: In-room Niceties. *Catering and Accommodation Management:* pp. 15, 17, August 1989.
West, J. J.: Competitive Tactics in Food Service. *Cornell Hotel and Restaurant Administration Quarterly:* pp. 68–71, May 1989.
Yesawich, C.: The Final Steps in Market Development: Execution and Measurement of Programs. *Cornell Hotel and Restaurant Administration Quarterly*: pp. 82–7, 89–91, February 1989.

Menus and Wine Lists
Bell, D.: Boosting Food and Beverage Profits. *Lodging Hospitality:* p. 57, May 1988.
Cohen, R.: The Leaner, Fitter Healthy Eating Sector. *London Restaurant Business*: pp, 10–12, 16 August 1988.
Dickens, J.: Less is More. *Catering and Accommodation Management:* pp. 13, 25, June 1989.

Dunk, S.: There's Profit in Vegetarian Food. *Publican*: pp. 14–15, 23 June 1988.

Helby, M.: Café-Bars and Brasseries. *Restauranteur*: pp. 80–2, November 1989.

Holland, R.: Seafood. *Pub Caterer*: pp. 29–30, 32, September 1988.

Ivory, M.: Salad Days. *Caterer and Hotelkeeper*: pp. 36, 40, 43, 46, 48, 15 September 1988.

Jameson, H: Shock Tactics Spanish Style. *Restauranteur*: p. 39, November 1989.

Martin, P.: Drinking Trends. *Restaurant Magazine*: pp. 20–1, November 1989.

Pettipher, L.: Staying Power. *Caterer and Hotelkeeper*: pp. 50–2, November 1989.

Rowe, D.: Wine — A Chilling Story. *London Restaurant Business*: pp. 20–2, 14 June 1988.

Rozario, K.: Function Catering. *Pub Caterer*: pp. 20–1, 24, September 1988.

Sutton, A.: Food Trends. *Restaurant Magazine*: pp. 24–6, November 1989.

Taylor, A.: The Early Bird Catches the Breakfast Trade. *London Restaurant Business*: pp. 18–19, 20 September 1988.

Thompson, J.: The Menu is the Key to Kitchen Planning. *Publican*: pp. 17, 18, 19, May 1988.

Wood, A.: Lager Clout. *Caterer and Hotelkeeper*: pp. 49, 50, 54–5, 14 September 1989.

Personnel

Ball, S. D., Johnson, K, and Slattery P.: Labour Productivity in Hotels: An Empirical Analysis. *International Journal of Hospitality Management*: Vol 5. (No. 3) pp. 141–7, 1986.

Cornell Hotel and Restaurant Administration Quarterly: Exit Interviews: How to Make a File Filler into a Management Tool. *Cornell Hotel and Restaurant Quarterly*: pp. 38–46, November 1987.

DeMicco, F. D.: Older Workers: A Hiring Resource for the Hospitality Industry. *Cornell Hotel and Restaurant Quarterly*: pp. 56–61, May 1988.

Pitfield, M.: Good Personnel Management Means Good Business. *National Westminster Small Business Digest*: pp. 1–4, July 1988.

Rowe, M.: Top Ten Traits of Good Employers. *Lodging Hospitality*: pp. 85–6, March 1989.

Whitney, D.: Focusing Attention on Your Waitstaff's Performance. *Cornell Hotel and Restaurant Administration Quarterly*: pp. 40–4, February 1989.

Woods, R. H.: Retention Programs That Work. *Cornell Hotel and Restaurant Administration Quarterly*: pp. 79–80, May 1989.

Restaurants

Castle, R.: A Bigger Pizza the Action. *Popular Foodservice*: pp. 30–1, 33, 34, 37, 38, September 1988.

Douglas, B.: Creating the Scene for Good Eating. *Catering in Scotland*: pp. 14–17, September 1988.

Garcia, M.: A Profit-sharing Plan for Restaurants. *Cornell Hotel and Restaurant Quarterly*: pp. 13–17, May 1989.

Harmer, J.: Berni: Fit, Lean and Ready for Growth. *Caterer and Hotelkeeper*: pp. 40–3, 29 September 1988.

Heathcote, E.: Catering in the Eighties, the Leisure Industry is set to Capture the Lions Share. *Leisure Business*: pp. 44–5, June 1988.

Lee, D. R. Factors in Restaurant Success. *Cornell Hotel and Restaurant Administration Quarterly*: pp. 32–7, November 1987.

Small Business

Ward, P.: Launching a Business. *Caterer and Hotelkeeper:* pp. 55, 59, 61, 22 September 1988.

Harmer, J.: The Chef Business. *Chef:* pp. 18–19, September 1988.

Horton, E.: How to Use Advertising to Develop Your Small Business. *Executive Post:* pp. 1, 6, 7, June 1989.

Lowe, A.: Small Hotel Survival — An Inductive Approach. *Hospitality Management.* Vol. 7 (No. 3), pp. 197–223, 1988.

Scoular, C.: Starting up a Business. *Restauranteur:* pp. 24–8, October 1989, and pp. 42–4, November 1989.

PART TWO

Case Studies

— 1 —

The Stagshead Hotel

Introduction

This case study demonstrates the value of accounting concepts, such as operational budgeting, establishment of cash flows and breakeven calculations, in a realistic scenario. It is a worked example and as such does not require you to answer questions. It should be used as an introductory case which is tutor led. From this case study you will understand how concepts, such as budgeting, relate to operational situations. It also introduces you to the techniques of comparative analysis through the use of published statistical material. To demonstrate this fully, the example is kept as simple as possible.

As in all the cases that follow only a limited amount of information can be provided. Thus there is a reliance on you to:

- Carry out research from published materials available

- Make assumptions where appropriate.

When assumptions are made, the onus is clearly on you to declare them and to explain your reasoning accordingly.

The purchase

Robert Camburn proposes to buy The Stagshead Hotel on 1 January 1991 from the current owner who is retiring. Preliminary market feasibility work carried out by a hired consultant suggests that the hotel has considerable potential for development, but Camburn and his consultant consider it is necessary to construct a number of budgets to verify this, and to ensure that the venture is a sound investment.

Purchase details

The Stagshead Hotel has ten single, six double and seven twin rooms, giving a total of 36 bed spaces available. It has a lounge bar with capacity for 70 covers and a restaurant with capacity for 45 covers. The purchase price for the property is £315,000, including fixtures and fittings valued at £45,000. Stock is valued at £22,000 and Camburn has agreed to accept this as part of the purchase. Camburn has £200,000 of his own capital and has secured a bank loan to cover the remainder of the purchase.

Preliminary estimates of sales and costs can be established using a variety of sources outlined below in addition to historical data on past operating performance.

Indeed, Camburn has been advised that using historical information from the hotel in isolation is not advisable. The reasons for this are twofold. Firstly, the reopening will initiate many changes in operations and, secondly, the previous owner appears to have let the business run down over the previous five years.

The average local room rate in 1990, for similar hotels, is £32 per person per night. In addition, a market survey undertaken in 1989 by the local tourist board indicated that an average yearly bed occupancy of 66 per cent can be anticipated in this busy tourist area.

The retaurant has proved popular in the past and the new owner intends to retain the menus and prices for the first year, after which new ideas will be introduced. Prices currently are: breakfast at £4.20, two-course lunch at £6.25, and three-course dinner at £8.60. Breakfast is not included in the accommodation tariff, and approximately 40 per cent of all overnight guests take breakfast. Lunch and dinner are currently one sitting. While the restaurant is almost always full at the weekend, the average daily covers for the past year are 19 at lunchtime and 27 at dinner. The bar sells no food but is popular with local residents and has had a steady turnover of approximately £3,000 per week for the past year.

From historical cost, market research, consultancy and examination of similar operations, the following variable expenses have been estimated and are shown as a percentage of departmental sales:

Cost of sales	Food	35%
	Beverage	37%
Direct labour	Rooms	15%
	Food	25%
	Beverage	20%
Other departmental expenses	Food	8%
	Beverage	8%
	Rooms	8%

Undistributed expenses (all fixed) are estimated as follows for the first year of trading (1991):

Administration and general	£ 9,384
Heat, light, power	£20,166
Marketing	£11,524
Property maintenance	£14,981

Fixed charges for the year are £120,000. The annual interest payments of the bank loan are at a rate of 15 per cent. From research and with the help of local consultancy services, Camburn has attempted to develop a pattern of sales and expenses within the business. Sales are likely to be slow to begin with as a new operation will take time to establish a reputation and build on the marketing efforts undertaken. Sales are expected to increase in the second and third quarters, as tourism statistics and historical trading data indicate that this is the busy period in this location and, accordingly, trade should increase. The final quarter, which is the low season, will see an estimated reduction in sales. For simplicity, all sales will be on a cash basis and direct costs will be paid as they accrue. All other expenses are estimated to be paid as follows:

Quarter	1	2	3	4
Sales	20%	30%	35%	15%
Administration and general	25%	25%	25%	25%
Heat, light, power	–	50%	–	50%
Marketing	50%	50%	–	–
Property maintenance	–	–	–	100%
Fixed charges	50%	–	–	50%
Interest on loan	–	–	–	100%

Construction of the trading and profit and loss account

From the information just outlined, Camburn can start to estimate for sales revenue from each department, and the cost information allows for the production of a summary trading and profit and loss account. When estimating sales there are clearly many limiting factors which can affect figures produced. Such factors include:

- The number of rooms in the hotel

- The number of seats in the restaurant

- The maximum capacity of the bar

- The hours of operation per day

- The days of operation per year

- The total customers available

- The maximum *practical* price

- The level of demand for each department.

Some of these variables are more or less certain — capacities of the facilities and days of operation, for example. However, others depend on estimates. The most important factor when estimating the value of any variable is to make maximum (but cost effective) use of available information to limit the guesswork involved. This information can come from several sources including historical data, market research, and consultants' reports. A useful technique is to calculate maximum possible revenue and then compare that with actual revenue for the Stagshead Hotel. This has revealed that actual food sales against total *potential* food sales were poor, for example.

In construction of the statements, several points must be taken into account. The pricing and marketing policies that may be adopted in a new operation can differ from those of an established unit. Hence year one projections may take into account promotional pricing, high initial marketing costs and small variances in budget targets until the business is running smoothly. The likely need for budget fine tuning, together with the possibility of early sales being erratic, should be noted.

Projecting room revenue for the Stagshead Hotel for year one:

Numer of beds × Rate × Days of operation in year × Expected occupancy

In order to fill in the variables, some use can be made of historical data in addition to published data from data collection agencies, which will provide borad averages for regions or types of hotel. These, together with appropriate local market research, should provide reasonably accurate information. After research, it can be assumed that the following variable values will have been obtained for The Stagshead Hotel. If the sleeper rate remains the same as the previous year, then the first three of the variables used here are certain. Only the expected occupancy of 66 per cent is likely to *actually* vary:

36 beds × £32 rate × 365 days × 0.66 occupancy = £277,517

Clearly, this is a simple example which ignores muliple room rates, double occupancy, discounting, etc, but it acts as a basis from which to work. Greater accuracy can be achieved if as many other contributing variables as possible are taken into account.

Food and beverage sales for year one can be calculated by a similar, but more problematic, method (more problematic because there are more variables, and seat occupancy, average spend and so on, are more difficult to estimate). However, information from the case can be used in the projection of food sales. The budgets have been set cautiously and no increase in the number of guests is expected over last year.

The following formulae are used for food and beverage revenue:

Breakfast revenue
40% of overnight guests × breakfast charge = 3,469 × £4.20 = £14,570

Lunch revenue
Guests per day × days of operation per year
× lunch charge = 19 × 365 × £6.25 = £43,344

Dinner revenue
Guests per day × days of operation per year
× dinner charge = 27 × 365 × 8.60 = £84,753

Beverage sales
£3,000 × 52 weeks = £156,000

This approach is also simplified, but it can act as a basis for refinement. As a check, projected food and beverage sales can be considered as a proportion of total sales by using industry statistics for rooms, food and beverage sales mix. If the estimates vary greatly from general industry norms, then projections should be reviewed. In the case of this hotel, the information sources indicate that the expected sales mix will be:

Rooms	48%
Food	25%
Beverage	27%

It is now possible to construct the trading and profit and loss account by taking together the revenue figures, and the expense estimates from the purchase details already given.

Projected Trading & Profit & Loss Account
for the Stagshead Hotel 1991

	Rooms £	Food £	Beverage £	Total £
Sales	277,517	142,667	156,000	576,184
Cost of sales	–	49,933	57,720	107,653
Gross profit	277,517	92,734	98,280	468,531
Direct labour	41,628	35,667	31,200	108,495
Dept expenses	22,201	11,413	12,480	46,094
Administration and general				9,384
Heat, light, power				20,166
Marketing				11,524
Property maintenance				14,981
Fixed charge				120,000
Interest				20,550
Net profit				£117,337

Construction of the cash flow forecast

For the sake of simplicity, the cash flow statement will be outlined by quarters and will ignore credit transactions. The budgeted cash flow statement can be produced by looking at the inflows and outflows of *cash* to and from the business and then determining the pattern of flow. The *sum* of inflows and outflows is largely determined by the information already prepared in the budgeted trading and profit and loss account, while the *pattern* of flow can be determined by research outlined under *Purchase details* (see page 37).

Budgeted cash flow statement for
the Stagshead Hotel

	1 £	2 £	3 £	4 £
Inflows				
Owners funds	200,000	–	–	–
Bank loan	137,000	–	–	–
Rooms revenue	55,503	83,255	97,131	41,628
Food revenue	28,533	42,800	49,933	21,400
Beverage revenue	31,200	46,800	54,600	23,400
Total inflows	452,236	172,855	201,664	86,428

	1	2	3	4
	£	£	£	£
Outflows				
Premises	315,000	–	–	–
Stock	22,000	–	–	–
Food cost	9,987	14,980	17,476	7,490
Beverage cost	11,544	17,316	20,202	8,658
Direct labour	21,698	32,548	37,973	16,274
Dept expenses	9,218	13,828	16,133	6,914
Administration and general	2,346	2,346	2,346	2,346
Heat etc	–	10,083	–	10,083
Marketing	5,762	5,762	–	–
Property maintenance	–	–	–	14,981
Fixed charges	60,000	–	–	60,000
Interest on loan	–	–	–	20,550
Total outflows	457,555	96,863	94,130	147,246
Surplus deficit	(5,319)	75,992	107,534	(60,818)
Balance B/F	–	(5,319)	70,673	178,207
Balance C/F	(5,319)	70,673	178,207	117,389

Breakeven analysis

The breakeven point (BEP) occurs when total costs are equal to total revenue. The breakeven point of the first year can be calculated as follows:

Total sales	= £576,184
Total variable cost	= £262,242
Total fixed costs	= £196,605
Net profit	= £117,337

Therefore the contribution (that is, total sales less total variable costs) to fixed cost and profit = £313,942

Contribution/Sales (C/S) ratio = 0.545

BEP (fixed costs C/S ratio) = 196,605 / 0.545 = 360,743 or 63 per cent of sales

The margin of safety is the difference between BEP sales and total sales.
Thus the margin of safety = 215,441 or 37 per cent of sales

The Stagshead Hotel can cover its fixed costs from 63 per cent of sales. This gives a wide margin of safety. If sales targets are not met, it is unlikely that the hotel will make a loss unless budgets are considerably overstated.

Summary

Subsequent years should take into account that the business should now be stable, and have built a level of repeat business and goodwill. If the hotel can secure dominance over certain market segments, then projected income and pricing policy should reflect this. External factors, inflation, general price changes and other variables should also be reflected and acknowledged. Over the next year, Camburn should aim to increase food and beverage sales and possibly increase the average sleeper rate without loosing occupancy.

This is a very simplified example. It does not take into account the effects of credit on cash flows and simplifies some of the variables used to determine figures. However, it forms a basis for the budgeting process for any establishment and allows a degree of forward planning to take place. Camburn now has the basis for the first year's operating budgets. He is able to monitor the critical early life of the business and will be able to assess the effectiveness of the operation by variance analysis. Budget projections would be constantly monitored for any variance, and the budget would either be modified to reflect greater realism, or the source of the variance from expected results investigated and rectified.

— 2 —

Special Events

Introduction

Margaret Hall and Robert McGoven have operated a small outside catering business, Special Events, in south London for the last five years (1985–9). Its steady growth and good reputation is based on a combination of hard work, cost control and considerable attention given by the partnership to customer care. From their current base in a small shop and kitchen area, the partners are keen to expand their current operation and are also considering diversifying by starting a fast-food, home delivery service. They are aware that considerable planning is required for these proposals and have asked you to assist. Initially, you need to provide:

1. An outline review of their current business.

2. Comment on the proposed expansion of existing business (Phase 1).

3. An outline of the planning required to diversify (Phase 2) and comment on the possible problems involved.

The following information should be used to form the basis of your report.

Overview

In 1984 Margaret Hall was working as an assistant manager with a fast-food company and Robert McGoven was working as a sous chef at a four-star, city centre hotel. Both had worked on a private basis for an outside caterer during their spare time and holiday periods. Out of this shared work experience grew the idea of setting up a partnership specialising in quality outside catering. They both gave up their jobs and took a lease on premises in January 1985 (see Appendix 4 for a plan of the premises). Special Events, as they called their partnership, was based upon standards and style of operation detailed below. While all legal requirements of business start-up were fulfilled, no detailed partnership agreement was drawn up as the couple had been good friends for a number of years, had plans to get married at some point in the future, and thus considered such formality as unnecessary.

The product

They started operating as an outdoor specialist catering service, providing customers with a degree of personal service and customer care intended to be higher than that provided by the larger contract/outside catering companies. Since the first year, they have changed their approach only slightly and still advertise locally. They give free advice to clients at all stages of the planning of each function to ensure the event will be both memorable and special. Normally, one or both of the partners visits the client on several occasions to finalise details.

Hall and McGoven's experience has told them that the presentation of food at an outdoor or nonhotel/restaurant venue has often been problematic for larger operators. According to them, competitors' presentation is often flawed and the service is erratic. They consider the vital factor in the success of Special Events is that the presentation and service of food and wine is of the highest standard. All food is presented simply on plain white crockery, all linen — from napkins to tableclothes — is made of the finest, starched Irish linen. Quality cutlery and sparkling glasswear are all part of the setting for that 'special event'. Name cards, table plans, etc, are often provided as part of the all-inclusive charge.

The business operates under the joint guidance of the partners and gives a 'chef-patron' feel to the event. Two 'core' staff are employed on a full-time basis (approximately 30 hours a week), who are supported by students from local hotel and catering colleges. All staff involved are briefed and 'trained' prior to each event. Staff are selected on the basis of their experience, expertise and ability to transfer enthusiasm to customer care. Such care, with the selection and training of staff, according to Hall, reflects Special Events' commitment to professionalism. There are strict standards for staff dress and grooming. All of the staff will work under the direct supervision of the proprietors.

The partners take the view that the essence of high quality food lies in the ingredients used and skills of the staff. Menus are composed by McGoven according to which produce is in season. Fresh produce is delivered daily to the kitchen. The menus shown in Appendix 1 are produced as samples of the 'type' they currently offer.

Functions have taken place at private homes, historic sites, country houses, museums, art galleries and even in aircraft hangers and warehouses. Contracts for catering at a private box at race meetings have recently been won, and this is seen as a growing area of business. Recently, one of these function menus was served to a small, but well connected, party at Aintree. The 'Grand National Winners Day Menu' was designed according to the specifications of the client, and the following services were included:

- Race cards and sporting newspapers
- Floral decorations
- Credit bar facilities
- Selected vintage wines and mineral water to accompany the meal.

This function, and the general feeling that growth should be the next major objective, has prompted the partners to consider expansion. However, they had different ideas on this matter. McGoven wished to expand the existing business, while Hall considered diversification into providing a home delivery service. After some heated exchanges, they agreed to compromise.

Phase 1: Expansion of Special Events

For business clientele requiring more than simply catering, Hall and McGoven have agreed that, from this year (1990), they will offer the following in addition to their existing services:

- Hire of venue

- Hire of syndicate rooms within hotels

- Hire of audio/visual equipment

- Secretarial services

- Photocopying, telex and fax services

- Portable telephones.

Special Events will also organise recreational aspects of meetings including: squash, tennis, hill walking, fishing, horse riding, golf, shooting and visits to cultural attractions.

At this stage, the owners do not propose to move premises, although this may become necessary if business expands beyond the limit of the current operating facilities (turnover is believed to be in the region of £100,000). The cost of new equipment is estimated at £19,000 — this is funded mainly out of retained profit (the bank will be approached for an overdraft if any cash shortfall exists). The majority of equipment will be hired from specialist companies and Hall is currently searching for suitable suppliers. According to her, the decision to hire rather than purchase is a sound one, as the initial cost is prohibitive and the bank would be unlikely to grant a loan for the proposed expansion.

Phase 2: To Develop a Fast-food Home Delivery Service

While the proprietors believe that to stay in outside catering is important, they take the view that a move into the fast-food home delivery service would be beneficial. A 24-hour delivery service, to be called 'Special Delivery Fast Foods', will operate with new vehicles from the current premises. By undertaking this diversification, Hall and McGoven expect to benefit in three distinct ways: first, to take advantage of the growing demand for this type of product; secondly, to maximise the operational productivity of their current premises — of ovens, fixtures and kitchen space, and staff time, for example; and thirdly, to minimise the effects of 'flat spots' in demand in one single sector.

The new venture will be developed and managed by Hall capitalising on her past experience of the fast-food industry. According to her, customers will be predominantly young people who will live or work within a 10 mile radius of the premises. Takeaway customers may also be catered for, as the forward section of the premises borders a busy main road and could be converted to a shop front with service counters. A new member of staff will be recruited for the service. The need for other staff will be reduced by using the Special Events staff during slack periods. In this way, they will make full use of their staff.

Margaret Hall has given a good deal of thought to this project and has considered the following ideas:

1. Great emphasis will be put on the quality of the delivery service. All delivery personnel will be uniformed and trained in service greeting, order provisions,

packaging, remittance advice and farewell. In this way, it is hoped to develop a unique delivery service.

2. A high level of attention will be given to product packaging, the display of the producty in the package, the prevention of deterioration in storage, and heat retention in transit. All package materials will detail the name and address and telephone number of Special Delivery Fast Foods.

3. All deliveries will contain a takeaway menu card, and personnel will be trained to promote repeat business, schedules orders, etc.

4. Slightly 'exotic' food will be offered to appeal to a more knowledgable and adventurous consumer. Thus the product will be somewhat different from the 'usual' home delivery service provided by others. An outline of the intended product range is given in Appendix 3.

The cost of this diversification has not yet been estimated, but it is hoped that much of it will be paid for out of retained earnings from the other part of the business. It is hoped that, by 1992, this side of the expansion can take place.

Appendix 1: Special Events — Sample Menus and Wine List

Menu 1: £23 per person including VAT

Sliced advocado salad with five beans and crispy gammon
served with mayonnaise and summer leaves.

Terrine of river salmon with tomato and almond dressing.

———

Fillet of sole filled with a light salmon and trout mousse
presented with a creamy dry martini sauce
with petals of saffron.

Fillet of beef, pan fried in herb butter presented with
a rich woodland mushroom and Madeira sauce.

A medley of fresh garden vegetables and potato.

———

Meringue and chocolate torte.
Lemon and manderine souffle.

———

Farmhouse cheeses with oatcakes.

———

Coffee.

Menu 2: £38 per person including VAT

Game and pheasant comsommé.

*Finest Scottish smoked salmon with
fresh lemon and brown bread.*

*Summer leaf delight with lobster, hazelnut oil, celeriac
and topped with crispy bacon.*

———

*Carved saddle of lamb
spread with a tomato and basil sauce,
and served with shallots and garlic bulbs.*

*Finest sirloin steak
cooked in a creamy burgundy sauce glazed with
fresh thyme and black pepper.*

*Dover sole
grilled or panfried in nutbrown butter.*

———

*Millefeuille of summer fruits
layered with chocolate and vanilla pastry.*

*Poached pears glazed under a strega sabayon with
a wafer tulip filled with water ices.*

———

*Selection of European cheeses
served with apple and celery.*

———

Coffee and Mints.

FINE WINE SELECTION CHART — SPECIAL EVENTS

CHAMPAGNE		
Pommery et Greno	NV	£29.50
Lanson	NV	£35.50
Moet et Chandon	NV	£29.00
CALIFORNIA WHITE		
Fume Blanc	1985	£17.00
AUSTRALIAN WHITE		
Chardonnay	1987	£14.00

BURGUNDY WHITE

Chardonnay	1986	£21.00
Chablis	1986/7	£29.00

LOIRE

Sauvignon de Tourraine	1987	£18.50
Sancerre	1987	£17.00

ALSACE

Riesling Reserve	1986	£11.00

ITALY WHITE

Orvieto Classico	1987	£15.00

HOUSE WINES

House Red	£12.00
House White	£12.00
Muscat de Beaume de Venise	£22.00

BORDEAUX

Chateau la Gardera	1985	£19.00
Chateau Haut Lignan	1981	£23.00

PAULLIAC

Chateau Grand Puy du Chasse	1981	£39.00

GRAVES

Chateau Millet	1980	£37.50

POMEROL

Chateau des Anneraux	1983	£29.50

BEAUJOLAIS

Brouilly	1987	£23.50
Fleurie	1987	£27.50

RHONE RED

Cotes de Rhone Villages	1986	£18.00

BURGUNDY RED

Santenay	1985	£25.00
Mercurey	1986	£20.00

ITALY RED

Chuanti Classico Reserva	1981	£14.50

Appendix 2: Special Events Summary of Financial Information to Date — Summary of Trading 1985–9

Year	Sales	Cost of sales	Labour*	Other variable	Fixed charges	Net profit
	£	£	£	£	£	£
1985	57,000	19,270	11,100	9,900	9,000	7,730
1986	59,500	19,000	12,040	10,115	9,100	9,245
1987	71,750	22,243	12,960	13,635	9,300	13,612
1988	77,000	25,410	14,640	13,000	9,600	14,350
1989	82,200	27,950	16,965	13,160	9,700	14,425

* This figure does not include any payment to the proprietors.

Appendix 3: Special Delivery Fast Foods — Outline of Proposed Product Range

Pizza Special
(Range of pizza sizes and toppings)

Sate Special
(Range of sate snacks with various sauces and accompaniments)

Tapas Express
(Range of authentic tapas snacks)

Mexican Special
(Range of Mexican fast-foods — enchillados, tortillas, burritos, etc)

Potato Express
(Range of filled jacket potatoes)

Shanghai Express
(Range of Chinese dishes, rice and other accompaniments)

All available 24 hours a day, 365 days per year — free delivery within a 10 mile radius.

Appendix 4: Special Events — Plan of Premises

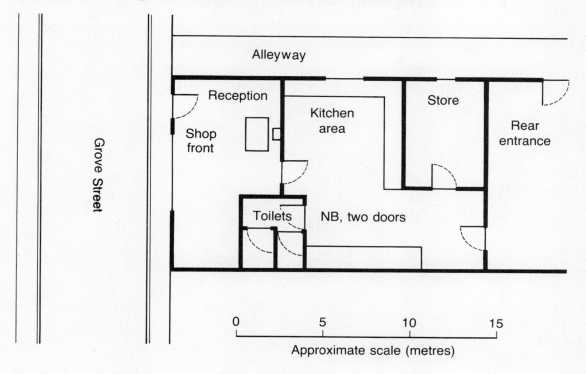

Alleyway

Reception

Shop front

Kitchen area

Store

Rear entrance

Grove Street

Toilets

NB, two doors

0   5   10   15

Approximate scale (metres)

Appendix 5: Special Events — Plan of Area

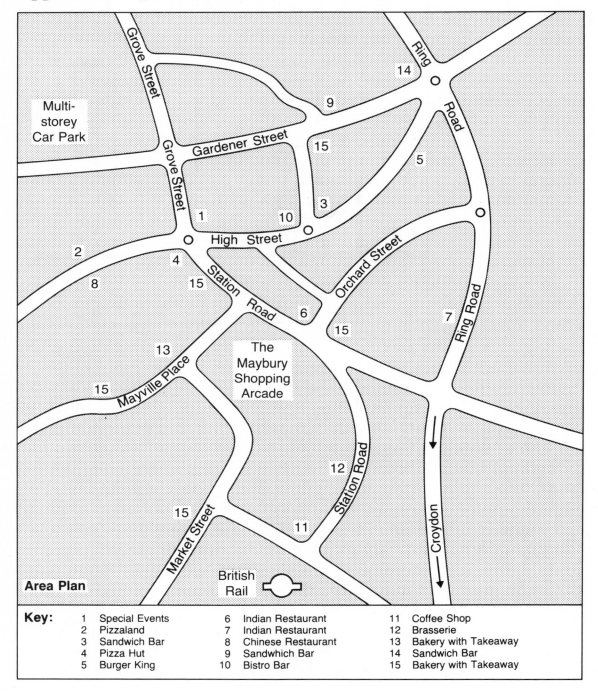

Key:					
1	Special Events	6	Indian Restaurant	11	Coffee Shop
2	Pizzaland	7	Indian Restaurant	12	Brasserie
3	Sandwich Bar	8	Chinese Restaurant	13	Bakery with Takeaway
4	Pizza Hut	9	Sandwhich Bar	14	Sandwich Bar
5	Burger King	10	Bistro Bar	15	Bakery with Takeaway

— 3 —

Europa Motels

Introduction

As operations controller for Europa Motels you are required to:

1. Review the operational problems 1988–9.

2. Offer suggestions for the future of the UK motels.

The background

Over the past five years, several European hotel/motel companies have expanded their Continental operations into the UK. In part, this was seen as a response to the increasing demand for low cost accommodation in busy business and tourist locations, and along major travel routes throughout the country. Preliminary findings published recently by an independent market research agency suggested that the demand for this type of accommodation will increase by 10 to 20 per cent by 1995. The research also noted that much of the increase would be net growth in demand rather than a shift in the preferences of existing consumers.

Europa Motels is a German motel and property group with 83 motels in Germany and France. The company has grown rapidly over the past seven years with an aggressive marketing policy and by undercutting most of its major competitors in room pricing. Motels account for 65 per cent of business and the remaining income is derived from a chain of nightclubs throughout Germany and from interests in construction companies. The construction company connection has allowed Europa to build motels in Europe at a cost 15 per cent less than major European competitors. However, for the construction of UK motels, it would be necessary to contract out the building work to local companies.

Three years ago, the board of directors noticed that a number of Continental rivals had expanded their operations into the UK. At the time, it seemed that none had a major market position and, on the advice of the marketing director, Europa decided to follow its competitors into what he considered to be 'a UK market ripe for development'. His researchers indicated the following:

- That the budget hotel market in the UK is currently dominated by traditional hotels either owned independently or as part of a major company.

- That the majority of group-owned hotels in this category are converted inns or private hotels accumulated over the years, and as such cannot compete with the purpose-built and highly-branded concept offered by Europa.

- That private bed and breakfast accommodation is not a threat.

The thrust of Europa's UK marketing strategy was that the company would offer very competitive tariffs on basic but good quality accommodation. To minimise cost, no support services would be included, such as restaurants or bars. Maximum use would be made of technology to minimise staffing requirements. The motels would be positioned strategically and would offer 'no frills', cut-price accommodation for the regular business client and for the budget tourist.

Several of the other directors did not share the optimism of the marketing director. In particular, reservations had been voiced about the possibility of obtaining adequate locations for the motels, and concern was expressed about the level of competition already in existence for this type of motel. Opinions were that the budget accommodation market in the UK was more complex than the marketing department suggested. Despite these reservations, the company decided to go ahead with the expansion programme, with two hotels being built in the first year and two in the second — all in England. Initial investments in each unit was approximately £700,000.

The UK motels

The UK office was established in London three years ago with an operations controller from head office. Other staff were recruited locally, including a marketing manager, a personnel and training officer and seven administration staff.

Numerous locations were considered for the new motels. Several prime properties were available, but appropriate greenfield sites were less common and were between 10 and 15 per cent more expensive than budgeted. Finally, after considerable searching and negotiation, the following locations were secured:

Motel 1: Harlow, Essex; 4 miles from the M11 motorway and 30 minutes from London; parking for 70 cars; 15 minutes' walk from the town centre.

Motel 2: Basingstoke, Hampshire, 2 miles from the M3 motorway and 1 hour 15 minutes from London; parking for 45 cars; town centre location.

Motel 3: Birmingham Central; parking for 25 cars.

Motel 4: Peterborough, Cambridgeshire, 2 miles from the A1 and 1 hour 30 minutes from London; parking for 60 cars; 20 minutes walk from the town centre.

The UK motels are similar to those on the Continent and are of prefabricated construction and, with minor exceptions, are based on a standard concept. Each motel is single storey and consists of 55 rooms, each room with a shower and bath. In addition, a two-bedroom management flat is combined with a small reception and office area.

Each room is large enough to accommodate one large double bed and each has an occassional foldaway bed stored in cupboard space. Facilities include a writing desk, colour TV, direct dial telephone and tea/coffee making facilities. At the reception, a photocopy machine is available for guest use during office hours.

On the Continent, Europa's motels have a semi-automated check-out and billing system that allows guests with approved credit cards to arrive and depart at any time without the need for reception staff. This system has not been adapted for the small number of UK hotels because of the prohibitive cost.

The small reception office is manned every day from 7.00 am to 7.00 pm. Outside these times, guests who require attention press a buzzer that sounds in the manager's flat. Each reception office is equipped with a small microcomputer that can take reservations up to a year in advance. The computer also has space for general guest history information but is not linked externally to any other system.

A central reservations office is based at the company's UK office in London. This comprises two assistants, working 9.00 am to 5.00 pm, Monday to Friday, taking and coordinating reservations by telephone. Each morning the central reservations office telephones each motel to advise them of advance bookings taken the previous day. Usually, these account for approximately 30 per cent of all bookings, while chance guests account for the remaining 70 per cent. To keep bookkeeping to a minimum, all guest accounts are settled upon departure and no deposit is required for advance bookings.

All the UK motels are run by management couples. Initially, couples who had worked for the company in Europe were brought in to start each unit. Eventually all four units were taken over by UK couples who had undergone a three-month training programme. Of the new management teams three were former public house tenants while the fourth had experience of large hotel management.

Each couple receives a set salary, free accommodation and a meal allowance. Management couples are allowed to hire personnel, and are required to train operational staff such as receptionists, cleaners and housekeepers. However, a budget limit is set for all direct costs by the operations controller. Maintenance and other general services are contracted out under agreement with the company. The management couples have no part in the hire of such contractors, but are obliged to report on the quality of work to the operations controller on a quarterly basis. All other fixed charges are controlled from the London office.

Pricing of rooms is based on a national tariff per room. Rates are intended to be lower than most major group competitors and no discounting is considered. The room rate for September 1990 was £27.50 per night.

The UK competitors

The competition for Europa Motels comes from a number of companies, both UK and overseas based. Europa's market researchers have identified competition from other modern, purpose-built motels and from several well-established, small hotel divisions of large companies.

In the purpose-built motel category, four significant competitors have been identified. Two companies concentrating on roadside motels built in close proximity to branded restaurants owned by the same company. Both of these companies have more than 30 motels. The other two, both European based, have grown by building budget hotels/ motels in a similar way to Europa, although normally larger in size and with restaurant facilities. They are mostly located in city centres or at airports. Both companies will have over 20 units by 1992.

According to the researchers, the competition from 'traditional' hotels is greater. They have identified five companies each with more than 60 'secondary' hotels. These are usually units with restaurant and bar operations as the major revenue earner, but with up to approximately 30 rooms. Often, these secondary hotel portfolios have been built up by the purchase of privately-owned hotels or coaching inns. Due to their established nature, such hotels are usually in prime locations.

Tariffs vary considerably between companies and between locations, but Europa has pitched its product at the lower price range and as a consequence, approximately two-thirds of all the competition noted above, have higher rack rates.

The current situation

Europa had been based in the UK for three years with two motels being built in each of the last two years. The board intended to increase the presence by two units in year three and by up to four per year over the next five years. Long-term objectives have not been fully articulated, but the general intention is to expand in the UK as far as the market would allow.

After a slow start in year one, a countrywide advertising campaign in selected business press resulted in improved occupancy. The results are summarised below.

ROOM OCCUPANCY PER QUARTER
(PER CENT)

Quarter	1	2	3	4
Year 1				
Motel 1	45%	57%	63%	61%
Motel 2	39%	56%	60%	60%
Year 2				
Motel 1	44%	59%	61%	59%
Motel 2	39%	54%	62%	61%
Motel 3	41%	45%	49%	53%
Motel 4	39%	48%	45%	39%

The mix of guests in year two was as follows (per cent per year):

	Business	UK tourists	Overseas tourists
Motel 1	74%	22%	4%
Motel 2	67%	31%	2%
Motel 3	69%	21%	10%
Motel 4	56%	36%	8%

Repeat business for the group was approximately 24 per cent in year two; while 74 per cent of guests settled their account by credit card, one-third of these were company expense cards.

Profitability percentages (at 14.5 per cent) have reached targets for the group in both years of operation. However, turnover has not reached budget in any of the motels, and the board has decided to review the UK operation. The unit management couples, the UK operations controller and senior corporate representatives met at one of the motels to examine the situation. After a review of the trading situation, the main items that were minuted during the meeting are summarised below:

Management couples felt that they had little control over the business except in minor day-to-day decisions. They also commented that the strict budget limits set for operational staff caused staff shortages and the inability to attract and retain good quality staff for operational tasks.

Management couples also complained about the level of no-show guests. A number of examples were cited of high potential occupancy being diminished by approximately 25 per cent of advance bookings not materialising.

The operations controller summarised information gathered from guest questionnaires that had been collected from guest rooms and had been forwarded, unopened, to him at head office. This policy has been in operations since the UK motels were built and was designed to give the coordinator an independent impression of the quality of service in each motel. Favourable comments were often noted about the quality of the motel rooms, the reasonable price and about the good parking facilities. However, numerous complaints were received about the lack of facilities during nonoffice hours and the attitude of some staff. Several unfavourable comments were also made about the reservations service, but such comments were not specific enough to draw conclusions. Other comments made reference to the quality of the competition, but few were specific.

Since the meeting, one of the management couples have resigned in order to return to being public house tenants. The vacancy of the Birmingham motel has yet to be filled.

— 4 —

Talbot Restaurant

Introduction

The Talbot Restaurant is the ground floor and cellar of a converted town house dating from the eighteenth century that has been operated for the past five years as a licenced restaurant. The current freeholders, Mr and Mrs Robinson, have decided that next year (1991) they will upgrade the business by improving the kitchen facilities, restaurant decor and by providing an improved menu and wine list to replace the current offerings.

The cost of upgrading the restaurant has been estimated at £28,000. Half of this can be met out of savings and the rest is to be borrowed from the bank. The small business advisor at the bank has indicated that an outline plan of operational intentions is required before the loan is granted. In particular, the plan must convince the bank that the business proposal is financially sound and that revenue will increase sufficiently to cover loan repayments.

You are required to:

1. Outline an overall strategy for the redevelopement of the restaurant, including revised menu and wine lists and a summary of operating budgets for 1991. This outline should be taken from the perspective of the Robinsons, and aimed at justification for being granted the bank loan.

2. Review the proposal from the perspective of the bank.

An overview

Over the past five years, the Robinsons have gradually increased their trade, and built a reputation as an honest, mid-priced restaurant (see Appendix 4). Traditional dishes figure strongly on the menu and are offered with a modest wine list comprising well-know table wines. Much of the trade comes from locals, passing tourists and, at the weekends, commuters from south London suburbs (see Appendix 5).

The decision to upgrade is based on two factors. First, the Robinsons are bored with the type of food they are producing and want to experiment with more complex dishes. They feel from experience that there is a demand for a higher quality operation. Indeed, many residents in the village itself, and in nearby commuter suburbs, are young professionals with high potential spending power. Second, there are no other quality restaurants in the village, although several of the chain-owned public houses and inns have food operations similar to that currently offered at the restaurant.

The area

The Talbot Restaurant is located in the village of Oxten (population 6000) in Surrey. The village is situated close to the M25 motorway and 1 hour and 25 minutes drive from Croydon. There are also several nearby towns and villages forming a substantial potential market for the restaurant. A high proportion of new residents are professional people, but the majority (about 4,000) have lived in the village for over ten years and are employed locally. It is estimated that more than 200,000 people live within two hours' driving time of the village. A summary of the Talbot Restaurant's guest information appears in Appendix 5.

The property

The restaurant is situated in the main street of the village and comprises a beamed dining area which can seat 65 customers, an extensive cellar (currently unused, and the same size as the restaurant), a modest kitchen and an adequate storage area. The decor and furnishings are in need of refurbishment and the kitchen is in need of some new equipment.

The product

The current menu and wine list are shown in Appendix 1. The restaurant is open from Tuesday to Sunday from 7.00 pm to 11.30 pm. Usually, there are two sittings, but when business is quiet, guests can take their time. Diners from Tuesday to Thursday tend to be locals and reservations rarely exceed 20 on each evening. However, Friday and Saturday evenings witnesses a large influx of people from further afield and often chance guests have to be turned away. Sunday evening tends to be unpredictable, bookings often depending upon social events taking place in the village.

The owners are helped by their daughter who is still at school, two part-time waitresses who live locally, and a general assistant who does the washing up, cleaning and some of the general maintenance. Staff training is provided informally by the owners during quiet evenings, but as all the staff have worked at The Talbot Restaurant for over a year, the need for training in recent times is percieved as minimal.

Mrs Robinson has recently started an evening class in advanced French cuisine at a London college and together with her husband's many years of experience in hotel management, expects to be able to cope with the more complex menu they have in mind. At this stage, they do not plan to employ a professional chef as this may prove expensive. However, if demand is great and maintained they intend to review the staff situation. In the meantime, a further two part-time waitresses will be employed when the new operation starts.

The competition

There are no privately-owned restaurants in the village offering high-quality French cuisine. Six chain-owned public houses or inns offer popular dishes, such as prawn cocktail, steak and gâteau. The Robinsons have visited all of these to make comparisons. They estimate a dinner spend of between £7 and £12 in each. Two of the six offer the same menu at lunch. Both appear to have a reasonable lunchtime trade and the Robinsons had considered competing for this business. However, Mr Robinson decided that he needed some time for leisure and that opening for lunch and dinner would mean a fourteen hour day, six days a week.

The other two pubs in Oxten are both privately owned and offer microwave bar snacks throughout the day. There is an Indian restaurant and a Chinese take away. However, there are not seen as rivals to The Talbot Restaurant as they are both priced at a considerably lower average spend. Nevertheless, the Indian restaurant has recently started to offer a two-course business lunch buffet style at £4.25. This has proved very popular to the extent that competitors offering pub-lunches have decided to consider new menus.

There is one chain-owned hotel in the village with 27 rooms, which together with guest house bed and breakfast accommodation brings the total number of bedspaces in Oxten to approximately 80.

In the next village, which is four miles away, is The Merlin. This restaurant has been run very successfully by the same owners for seven years, and has attracted much of the high-spend custom in the locality. In recent years, it has benefited from several favourable reports in local and national gourmet press. The restaurant specialises in freshly caught fish and local game, and the chef imports certain products directly from France on a weekly basis. Average spend at The Merlin is approximately £19.50 excluding wine. The menu at The Merlin is changed each month and is often supplemented by speciality menus at the weekend. A copy of the most recent speciality menu appears in Appendix 2.

In the same village as The Merlin, Dino's wine bar has attracted considerable business from Oxten residents, and is normally very busy most evenings but full to capacity from Thursday to Sunday night. The wine bar list is shown in Appendix 3. The owners of the wine bar are opening a bistro next door to The Talbot Restaurant in the next few months. This will have a simple, but well-designed menu with average prices of main dishes probably in the region of £4 to £6. The beverage list will be the same as in the wine bar and comprise carefully-selected, mid-priced wines.

Within a ten mile radius of The Talbot Restaurant there are three other villages of similar size to Oxten, and a town with a population of 45,000. In this area there are five other restaurants similar in quality to that to which the Robinsons aspire excluding The Merlin. The same radius includes seventeen mid-range restaurants (excluding those in Oxten) that approximate the level and style of The Talbot Restaurant as it operates currently. Wine bars in the area (excluding Dino's) total six.

Operating information for the redeveloped Talbot Restaurant (1991)

The Robinsons intend to operate the current menu and wine list for most of the current year (1990), and close the restaurant for November and December of 1990 for the refurbishment to take place. Reopening will take place in the first week of January 1991. The £14,000 from the bank loan is anticipated in mid-January 1991 and when this is received the full cost of the refurbishment will be paid to the contractors. Preliminary operational planning undertaken by the owners is as follows:

1. An average spend of £13 on food and £2 on wine is anticipated from the new menu and wine list.

2. The new menu will be à la carte and revisions will be made when necessary. The Robinsons intend to make greater use of local and seasonal produce.

3. The Robinsons have budgeted for an average of 30 covers per evening, operating for the same 297 days a year as operated currently (this takes into account six day opening, closing for summer holidays, and Christmas and New Year).

4. Expenses for the coming year are expected to be as follows:

Food and beverage cost: 36% of food and beverage sales (paid monthly)

Labour costs (fixed):

	Jane Robinson (daughter)	£1,500
	4 part-time waiting staff	£5,200 (each)
	1 general assistant	£6,000
	Mr and Mrs Robinson	£8,500 (each)

Sundry administration cost: variable at 7% of total sales (paid monthly)

Energy cost: variable at 4% of total sales (paid bimonthly)

Advertising: fixed charge of £2,200 pa (paid quarterly)

Repairs and maintenance (by fixed contract): £90 per month

Loan repayments: £3,500 pa for the next four years (paid each December)

Interest on loan: £130 pa for the next four years (paid in January)

Rates and other fixed charges: £9,800 pa (paid biyearly in June and December).

Appendix 1: The Talbot Restaurant — Current Menu and Wine List

STARTERS

Country Style Home Made Soup
Prawn Marie Rose
Brussells Paté
Chilled Melon with Smoked Ham
Seafood Cocktail

MAIN DISHES

All served with Potato and Seasonal Vegetables
Sirloin Steak
8 oz Steak with Pepper, Wine, Mushroom or Italian Sauce

Chicken Kiev
Baked Gammon with Pineapple
Traditional Lasagne
Roast Duck with Orange Sauce
Chefs Special Salad
Vegetarian Dish of the Day

DESSERTS

Selection of Ices
Selection of gâteaux
Profiteroles with Chocolate Sauce
Cheese and Biscuits

COFFEE

Regular or Speciality

Price: £11.50 including service and VAT

WINE LIST

RED WINES
House Red Wine (by the Glass or Bottle)
House Claret
Cotes Du Rhone
Beaujolais Villages
Bardolino
Chianti Classico
Californian Cabernet
Bulgarian Merlot

WHITE AND ROSÉ WINES

House White Wine (by the Glass or Bottle)
Muscadet de Sevre et Maine
Corbieres Blanc
Piesporter
Liebfraumilch
Lambrusco Bianco
Asti Spumante
Anjou Rosé

Appendix 2: The Merlin — Specimen Speciality Menu

Price £25.00

Poached Pear With Walnut and Calvados Sauce

———

Mousse of Salmon with a Light Avocado Sauce

———

Champagne Sorbet

———

Roast Quail
Bouquetiere of Fresh Local Vegetables
Roast and Parsley Potatoes

———

Selection of French Country Cheese

———

Coffee and Petit Four

Appendix 3: Dino's Wine Bar — Current Wine List

WINE LIST

FRENCH

House Wines	By the bottle	By the glass
House Claret, Bordeaux AC	8.20	1.55
Les Chais Rouge	7.55	1.55
La Bordelaise Blanc	7.55	1.55

Sparkling	Bottle	½ Bottle
Moet et Chandon Premiere Cuvee, N.V.	21.85	–
Veuve de Vernay Brut	14.90	–
Asti Spumante	11.50	–

Bordeaux Red		
Saint Emelion, A.C.	9.70	–
Medoc, A.C.	8.75	–
Chateau d'Angludet Cru Exceptional	13.60	–

Bordeaux White		
La Flora Blanc, Premiere Cotes de Bordeaux	8.95	–
Clos Saint Georges, Graves Superieur	12.70	–

Burgundy Red		
Macon Rouge, A.C.	8.70	–
Cotes de Beaune Villages, A.C.	10.80	–

Burgundy White		
Macon Blanc Villages, Moreau et Fils, 1985	10.40	–

Loire		
Anjou Rose, A.C.	8.80	–
Muscadet Serve et Maine	8.25	–
Poully Fume, Domaine Mauroy, 1985	11.75	–

Rhone		
Cotes Du Rhone (red or white)	9.70	–
Chateauneuf du Pape, A.C.	11.10	–

Alsace		
Gewurztraminer, A. Willem	9.95	–

GERMAN

Rhine		
Liebfraumilch, Qba.	8.80	–
Bereich Nierstein, Rheinhessen Qba.	9.10	–

Mosel		
Piesporter, Michelsberg Qba.	9.45	–
Bereich Bernkastel	9.44	–

ITALIAN
Chianti Classico (red or white)	11.75	–
Orvieto Classico Secco, 1985	10.35	–
Soave	8.90	–
Frascati Secco	12.00	–

SPANISH
Rioja Alta, Alberdi, 1978/80	12.75	–

PORTUGUESE
Vinho Verde. Alianca	12.75	–

YUGOSLAVIAN
Lutomer Laski Riesling	9.25	–

GREEK
Demestica, Red	8.25	–

ENGLISH
Chiltern Valley Riesling	11.10	–

AUSTRALIAN
Cabernet Sauvignon	9.05	–

LOW ALCOHOL AND DE-ALCOHOLISED WINE
Iceburg	6.90	–
Lambrusco Light (red, rosé or white)	6.90	–

BEERS AND SPIRITS
A selection of American and Continental beers and spirits are available – as advertised on the blackboard.

Appendix 4: The Talbot Restaurant — Summary of Covers Sold, Sales, Gross Profit Labour Cost and Net Profit (1986 to 1990)

	1986	1987	1988	1989	1990*
Covers sold	9,920	10,540	11,345	13,900	12,100
Sales revenue	£69,450	£75,880	£91,900	£112,850	£98,300
Gross profit	£44,448	£49,322	£59,735	£ 74,481	£64,900
Net profit	£ 4,862	£ 6,070	£ 9,185	£ 13,542	£11,800

* The figures for 1990 are extimates and include trading for ten months (January to October prior to closure.

Appendix 5: The Talbot Restaurant — Guest Information (1989)

The information was collected by the proprietors by discreetly asking guests to complete a simple questionnaire after their meal – 22 per cent of guests obliged. All figures are percentages of total respondents.

Guests from within 5 mile travelling distance	31%
Guests who have travelled 5 to 9 miles	22%
Guests who have travelled 10 to 14 miles	39%
Guests who have travelled more than 15 miles	80%
Guests arriving by car	83%
Repeat guests	61%
Guests in groups of three or more	32%
Guests under 30 years of age	19%
Guests over 30 years of age	48%
Groups of guests of mixed ages	33%

— 5 —

St Lambert College

Introduction

St Lambert College is a teaching college situated just outside of York. For the past three years the college holidays have provided an opportunity for the management to rent empty college residential accommodation and make a considerable contribution to year round running costs. Yet recently the revenue earning capacity of the vacation accommodation and catering facilities has begun to diminish, and budgets are not being matched with performance.

As an assistant consultant with Arrow Catering Consultancy Services, you have been asked to provide a cost-effective action plan to improve revenue earning capacity for the year 1991–2. Your report should:

1. Encompass an analysis of the current product being sold, and the deficiencies and weaknesses recognised.

2. Give a set of recommendations in the form of an action plan listing key areas requiring improvement, further investigation, and so on.

   Your report should comprise no more than 2,000 words exclusive of appendices.

Facilities

The college is set in 24 acres of its own grounds, five miles from York. It is a residential college, which has 80 study bedrooms; a lounge library; a gymnasium; a swimming pool; a 75 seater restaurant; and a 40 seater bar (Alberts), which serves snacks at lunchtime and dinner. Menus and wine lists for the restaurant and bar are included in Appendix 2. The grounds are landscaped and are open to guests throughout the vacation periods. The college is well signposted and within easy travelling distance of York. Major motorways are within a close radius, although rail connections are infrequent and are likely to be reduced in the near future. Room decor is somewhat dated, although the overall condition of the rooms is satisfactory. Pricing of residential accommodation during vacation periods is shown in Appendix 1.

A typical study bedroom consists of a single bed, a hand basin, and a WC and shower/bathroom attached. Furnishings include a chest of three drawers and a free standing wardrobe. The house is of an unusual Georgian design and after conversion, 50 of the bedrooms are situated on the ground floor with the remaining 30 situated on the first floor. The restaurant is also on the ground floor, and the wine bar is in a conservatory. Kitchens and storage facilities are located in the converted stables and outhouses at the rear of the building.

Occupancy

The major limitation on the scale of commercial bed space at St Lambert College is the length of the academic terms. Term dates are provided below and it is only during vacations that college accommodation can be let:

Academic Year 1990–1

First term
Friday 28 September 1990 to Friday 21 December 1990

Second term
Monday 7 January 1991 to Friday 22 March 1991

Third term
Monday 7 April 1991 to Friday 14 June 1991

The following represent weekly accommodation room occupancy percentages for academic year 1989–90, with budgeted figures in brackets. The budgeted accommodation for 1990–1 is also shown.

ACCOMMODATION OCCUPANCY PERCENTAGE (1989–90)

Week commencing	Occupancy %	Budgeted occupancy %
Summer term 1989		
19 June	20	60
26 June	25	65
3 July	30	70
10 July	77.5	75
24 July	70	80
31 July	72.5	80
7 August	85	85
14 August	90	90
21 August	92.5	100
28 August	90	95
4 September	90	100
11 September	87.5	100
18 September	80	100
Winter term 1989–90		
18 December	15	55
25 December	College closed	
1 January	College closed	
Spring term 1990		
19 March	25	60
26 March	20	65
2 April	37.5	75
9 April	42.5	75

BUDGETED ACCOMMODATION OCCUPANCY
PERCENTAGES 1990–1

Week commencing	Budgeted occupancy %
Summer term 1990	
25 June	50
2 July	55
9 July	60
16 July	85
23 July	90
30 July	95
6 August	100
13 August	100
20 August	100
27 August	100
3 September	100
10 September	100
17 September	
Winter term 90	
24 December	College closed
31 December	College closed
Spring term 1991	
25 March	55
1 April	65

Marketing Campaign 1989–90

In reponse to what was percieved as unrealised potential, the college joined an educational marketing consortium at a cost of £950 for one year's membership. The consortium provides a central reservations office charging 10 per cent commission for every reservation made. In return, the college is featured in the consortium brochure, which is mailed to all past customers of the consortium and selected groups of potential customers who have been identified by the consortium market research team. In total, consortium reservations accounted for 23 per cent of bookings in 1989–90, and the college's sub-committee for catering and accommodation have indicated some dissatisfaction with this, although it has been agreed that the college will retain consortium membership for a further year (1990–1).

Other marketing has been largely left to the accommodation manager who, although lacking in formal training, had begun to develop a systematic approach to marketing the college. She was considering joint ventures with a variety of organisations providing summer/winter school language training breaks for foreign students and low-spend overseas tourists who want to learn the English language. Although such business was likely to bring in 20 per cent less than the traditional vacation residents, it was still seen as a significant segment of the accommodation market to aim for.

Over the last six months the amount of time the accommodation manager has been able to devote to the task of marketing has been considerably affected by the college's inability to find replacements for staff who have either retired or left. Currently, four vacancies exist, all of which are within the accommodation section, and this has put considerable strain on remaining staff to ensure that all duties are fulfilled. Hence the college's decision to retain consortium membership since which constitutes the only major investment in the area of marketing in the past two years.

Personnel

The college management has delegated the operation of catering and accommodation, including vacation sales, to a controller of accommodation and catering. This person is responsible for the achievement of budgeted targets and the operational management of education and vacational letting. Budgets are developed by a sub-committee of the academic council on the basis of a report and summary, submitted each year by the controller of accommodation and catering. Ultimately, the controller must answer to the principal and the academic council, although in operational management of the facilities, considerable freedom exists. The management structure of the accommodation and catering facilities is given below.

Organisational Chart: Catering and Accommodation Services

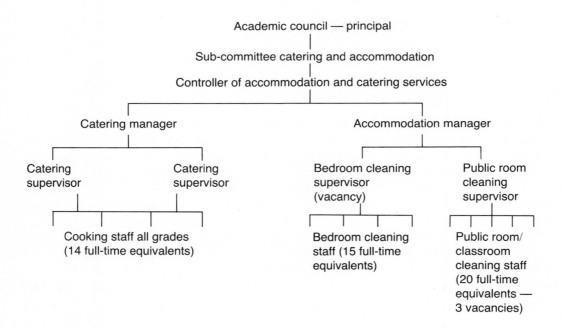

Accommodation Staff

The core of accommodation staff consists of female part-time workers employed from the nearby housing estates. These women provide a relatively reliable, flexible source of labour whose training requirements are usually of quite a low level. The majority of workers are unskilled and any cleaning training that is required is usually carried out in the workplace by the appropriate supervisor. It should be noted that currently there are three vacancies for part-time accommodation staff.

Catering Staff

Of the catering staff employed, 30 per cent are full-time while 70 per cent are part-time. These employees are responsible for the provision of all staff, student and vacation guest catering. Most of the staff receive a combination of on-the-job and off-the-job training, and recently the controller has been considering sending some of the cooks to the local catering college to undertake craft courses as part of their development and hopefully to improve food quality. Currently, a full-time vacancy exists for one of the catering supervisory posts. This post has been vacant for the past four months and the other full-time catering supervisor has complained that her tasks have become increasingly more difficult to perform to the standard required.

St Lambert College payment structure (1990)

No of staff	Post	Grade	Salary £	Live in
1	Catering and accommodation controller		13,575	
1	Catering manager		9,050	×
1	Accommodation manager		9,050	×
1	Catering supervisor		6,530	×
1	Catering supervisor (vacancy)			
1	Bedroom cleaning supervisor		7,390	×
1	Public room cleaning supervisor		7,090	×
1	Catering staff (full time)	I	6,290	
2	Catering staff (full time)	II	10,450	
1	Catering staff (full time)	III	4,950	
7	Catering staff (part time)	III	23,310	
0		IV		
2	Cleaning staff (full time)	I	9,850	
3	Cleaning staff (full time)	II	14,589	
0	Cleaning staff (full time)	III		
17	Cleaning staff (part time)	IV	39,204	
10	Cleaning staff (part time)	III	19,600	
	Total wages cost		£ 180,928	

Consumer satisfaction

As a result of various indications of dissatisfaction with service in the college, the controller last year carried out some research on the level of customer satisfaction. The following results were produced:

CONSUMER SURVEY RESULTS (1989)

Response rate	41%
Date of survey	Summer vacation 7–27 August
Average occupancy at time of survey	89.2%

Degree of satisfaction
Accommodation	67% dissatisfied
	28% satisfied
Food	81% dissatisfied
	15% satisfied
Liquor	10% dissatisfied
	72% satisfied

Treatment by staff
Reception/ reservations	22% high level of service
	65% average level of service
	13% low level of service
Housekeeping	0% high level of service
	14% average level of service
	70% low level of service
Food service	10% high level of service
	66% average level of service
	14% low level of service
Liquor service	14% high level of service
	57% average level of service
	13% low level of service

Appendix 1: St Lambert College — Pricing of Residential Accommodation

Accommodation Pricing

1989–90	£17.00 (adult)
	£ 7.00 (child under 12)
	£ 3.00 breakfast
1990–1	£19.50 (adult)
	£ 8.00 (child under 12)
	£ 3.50 breakfast

Appendix 2: St Lambert College — Menus and Wine List

A LA CARTE

HOUSE PÂTÉ £2.00
*Our Pâté is prepared daily and served
with French Bread*

GUACAMOLE DIP £2.25
*Fresh whipped Avocados served with
hot Pitta Bread and Crudites*

GARLIC BREAD £0.85
*Two pieces of French Bread toasted
and soaked in Garlic Extract*

SOUP OF THE DAY £1.95
*Fresh homemade soup served with
French Bread*

PRAWN COCKTAIL £2.00
*Prawns covered in our homemade
Seafood Sauce served on a bed of Iceburg
Lettuce with French Bread*

TARAMASOLATA DIP £2.25
*Puree of Cod's Roe served with
hot Pitta Bread and Crudites*

AVOCADO PRAWN £2.50
*Fresh skinned Avocado stuffed with
peeled Prawns in Seafood Dressing*

AVOCADO VINAIGRETTE £1.75
*Fresh skinned Avocado and help yourself
to our homemade sauce*

FROM THE GRILL

ENTRECOTE STEAK £8.50
The favourite steak of the French

LAMB CUTLETS £6.50
Three cutlets of best end of English Lamb

8oz BEEFBURGER £3.75
Delicious Prime Beef — A genuine Burger!

15oz T-BONE STEAK £9.00
*Best quality Scottish Beef — a real
plate-filler*

LA BROCHETTE £6.50
*Choice cuts of Leg of English Lamb
cooked on a skewer*

BURGER TOPPINGS £0.50
Choose from Cheese, Bacon, Chilli Each
or Sour Cream

All the above grills served with Pommes Frites

SNACKS AND DESSERTS

B.L.T. £2.50
*Grilled Bacon, fresh Iceberg Lettuce & Tomato
wrapped in hot Pitta Bread*

BAKED POTATO SPECIALS
*A large oven baked potato stuffed with
a filling. Choose from Cheddar Cheese,
Tuna Fish, Prawns & Seafood Dressing,
Chilli, Sour Cream.
(All served with fresh salad)*

DESSERTS £2.00   **COFFEE** £0.80
*A fresh selection daily of
desserts and exotic ice creams.*

STEAK SANDWICH £4.25
*A Minute Steak straight from the grill
wrapped in Pitta Bread*

CHILLI CON CARNE £4.50
A bowl of Chilli served with French Bread

CHEESE £1.95
*Choose from Cheddar, Camembert,
Stilton or Babybel, Served with French
Bread or Biscuits.*
Extra pieces £0.85
Per piece

ALL PRICES INCLUDE VAT AT 15% - SERVICE NOT INCLUDED

WINE LIST

White		Red	
Vin de Maison	5.95	Vin de Maison	5.95
Chardonnay Classique	8.50	Cote du Roussillon	6.50
		Cabernet Sauvignon	6.50

Burgundy

		Burgundy	
Bourgogne Grand Ordinaire	8.50	Bourgogne	8.50
Macon Villages Pinot Chardonnay	11.50		
Chablis 1988	14.95		

Beaujolais

Bordeaux		Beaujolais	8.50
Sauvignon	7.50	Fleurie	14.95
		Brouilly	11.95

Loire		**Rhone**	
Muscadet de Serve et Maine	6.95	Cotes Du Rhone	7.95
Sancerre 1987/88	13.95		
Vouvray 1987/88	7.95		

Bordeaux

Alsace		Club Claret	6.95
Pinot Blanc 1987	8.50	Medoc	7.50

Vintage 1984/85

Spain & Portugal		Chateau Latour	12.50
Vino Verdi	8.25	Chateau Gran Mazarolles	12.00
Siglo Saco 1987	8.50		

Italian & Spanish

Italian		Siglo Saco	8.50
Frascati	8.25	Lambrusco	6.50
Pinot Grigio	7.95		
Lambrusco	6.50		
Soave	5.95		

Half Bottles

German		Club Claret	3.95
Leibfraumilch	6.50	Beaujolais	4.25
		Cote du Rhone	4.25

Rose D'Anjou	6.95	**By the Glass**	
		Vin de Maison	1.30
		Cabernet	1.40
Half Bottles		Club Claret	1.50
Macon Villages	5.95	Beaujolais	1.70
Muscadet De Sevre et Maine	3.75	Siglo	1.70
Blanc de Blanc	3.50		
		Spritzer	1.60
By the Glass		Kir	1.70
Vin de Maison	1.30	Kir Royale	2.20
Chardonnay	1.70		
Sauvignon	1.50		
Muscadet	1.40		

		Champagne & Sparkling Wine	**Bottle/Glass**
Vino Verdi	1.70	House Champagne	16.95/3.50
Leibfraumilch	1.40	Verve Arnaud	8.50/1.80
Rose	1.50		

ALBERTS
BAR

Today's Specials

Soup of the day	1.95
Deep fried Courgettes or Mushrooms with garlic dip	2.50
Crispy Potato shells with	
Bacon	2.25
Bacon and Cheese	2.50
Chilli Con Carne	2.85
Grilled Trout coated inside with orange garlic butter served with Salad or Pomme Frites	7.50
Plaice pan fried in oil, lemon and capers served with Pomme Frites	7.50
Lamb chops served with Ratatouille and Pomme Frites	6.35

Today's Specials

— 6 —

Diamond Leisure

Introduction

Recent activity in the field of leisure and recreation has led to the growth of a number of new companies who are competing with two or three major operators who dominate the market. Certain new companies, who have acquired sites and outlets during the late 1980s are facing problems of recruitment and retention of staff. One such company is Diamond Leisure plc. The company was formed in 1986 with the aim of creating a broadly-based leisure corporation with holdings across the complete range of leisure outlets.

In the first four years of trading the company acquired fifteen new locations. The portfolio of business includes: nightclubs, leisure centres, amusement arcades, health and beauty outlets, casinos, nursing and old people's homes, and a number of seaside piers at minor UK resorts. The diversity of the outlets has made it difficult for the company to establish a brand or recognisable corporate image, which has resulted in it remaining relatively unknown outside the tourism and leisure industries.

The company's financial position over the past three years is summarised in Appendix 1.

As a member of DLR Consultancy Services you have been given the following brief on Diamond Leisure plc. Your task is to:

1. Review the corporate image of the company.

2. Review the unit management structure and management benefits.

3. Develop a recruitment and retention strategy for unit management and unit trainee management (your brief should include development and training details where appropriate).

4. Analyse the financial position of the company in view of the company's expansion plans.

Your response should take the form of a management report and consist of no more than 2,500 words exclusive of appendicies and graphics.

Company objectives

The company aims to become a major force in leisure management in the UK and Europe. The company takes the view that people's lifestyles are in a transition period. In recent years, leisure time has become central to the lives of many people — an identifiable experience with a great many ways in which it can be spent.

Diamond Leisure takes its environmental responsibilities seriously. Throughout all of its holdings, it has been policy to ensure that developments are in sympathy with local feelings, and the corporation is keen to take advice from, and to work with local authorities.

Company expansion

The company takes the view that the leisure and recreation market in the UK and Europe offers limitless oppportunities for growth. The product has considerable variety including: accommodation, food, refreshment, and the environment, which are provided with creativity and quality in mind.

A number of key areas for expansion have been identified:

- Hotel, restaurant and leisure outlets in dockland redevelopment sites in the UK.
- Nightclub and discotheque developments in France, Belgium and the Netherlands (USA theme in all outlets).
- Tenpin bowling clubs and ice-skating rinks in France and West Germany.
- Private nursing homes in the UK.
- Health and fitness clubs in provincial towns in the UK.

Expansion is planned strategically, and is not merely a response to development opportunities becoming available. Diamond Leisure recognises the requirement for planned growth and diversification.

Major competitors

The UK leisure market is dominated by major players, such as Mecca Leisure and First Leisure. Such companies must be seen as competitors and, to some extent, predators. Other companies include European Leisure, Whitegate Leisure and Themes International.

However, the growth of companies in this sector is rapid, and demand and supply in the market place is being examined and analysed continously by Diamond Leisure's head office.

Company organisation

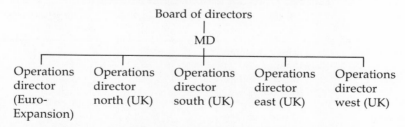

Organisation Chart Diamond Leisure plc

The operations directors are aided in their task by a personnel and training manager and a marketing manager. In total, some 458 employees work for Diamond Leisure. Some 39 are involved in managerial functions.

Company portfolio

The company's portfolio includes:
- 3 amusment centres (coastal resorts UK)
- 13 discotheques (provincial towns UK)
- 5 private nursing homes (provincial towns UK)
- 3 bowling alleys
- 4 casinos/night clubs (UK provincial towns)
- 3 seaside pier amusement complexes.

Mission statement

Attention to the needs of guests is the focus of Diamond Leisure. To constantly strive for greater standards of customer care and quality of service.

Personnel and development

At the head office of Diamond Leisure are people with expertise in the fields of leisure and recreation operations management and financial management. The aim has been to retain top level management, particularly during the expansion period of the company. In the UK, a difficulty has been identified at unit level concerning the recruitment of management of the right calibre. Although operations divisions have remained profitable, staff discontent has become apparent (labour turnover is detailed in Appendix 2). Furthermore, difficulties have arisen at trainee management levels.

A major problem with managerial staff is that they are being poached by competitors who believe that Diamond Leisure staff are very competent and an asset to any business. Another problem relates to the age of managers. As they become older, marry, and have children, the prospect of managing a casino, late-night amusement centre or nightclub becomes less attractive. Promotion within the company — out of operations and into area management — is notoriously slow, and the company has, in recent years, resorted to 'headhunters' and recruitment agencies to obtain area and head office staff. The motivation of unit managers may have been affected by this.

At trainee/assistant manager level, there appears to be difficulty in retaining staff. The company has tended to recruit individuals aged 25 or over with hotel or catering experience. However, retention of such individuals has proved a problem, and the average length of service for all management posts is listed by division:

SUMMARY OF RETENTION RATES — DIAMOND LEISURE PLC

Division	Post	Average length of service in years (max 4 years)
Amusement centres	Trainee manager	2.2
	Manager	4
Discotheques	Trainee manager	1.2
	Manager	3.1
Nursing homes	–	Purchased 1989
Bowling alleys	Trainee manager	2.1
	Manager	3.6
Casinos	Trainee manager	1.1
	Manager	3.1
Piers	–	Purchased 1990

Recently, recruitment of trainee managers has become even more difficult, and analysis carried out by a recruitment company indicated that the reasons for this are are follows:

- The low number of graduate/HND applications is due to the negative perception of night club/casino work.

- The high profile demanded of trainee/assistant managers.

- The perceived low status of bowling alley and amusement centre work among the potential managerial workforce.

Senior management accept these findings and realise they are facing a serious problem with unit management. A series of recommendations for immediate implementation are required.

Appendix 1: Diamond Leisure plc — Summary of Financial Position 1987–9

SUMMARISED BALANCE SHEETS FOR YEARS ENDING 1987–9 (£000)

	1987 £	1988 £	1989 £
Fixed assets			
Land and buildings	5,843	5,423	8,240
Plant and equipment	607	800	1,454
	6,450	6,223	9,694
Current assets			
Stock	17	85	165
Debtors	317	322	668
Cash	2,290	923	2,166
	2,624	1,330	2,999
Current liabilities			
Creditors	327	491	838
Short-term loans	2,340	2,170	5,711
	2,667	2,661	6,549
	(43)	(1,331)	(3,550)
	6,407	4,892	6,144
Long-term liabilities			
long-term loans	55	523	2,810
Shareholders equity			
Ordinary share capital	6,352	4,369	3,334
Trading information	87	88	89
Sales	6,028	6,531	11,446
Net profit	1,261	477	106

Appendix 2: Diamond Leisure plc — Labour Statistics

TOTAL LABOUR TURNOVER
BY DIVISION (UK)

Division	1988 %	1989 %
Discotheques	34	49
Nursing homes	10	14
Bowling alley	36	39
Casinos	42	49
Pier complex	39	38
Amusement centres	31	34

— 7 —

Glenlarch Country House Hotel

Introduction

Glenlarch Country House Hotel and Leisure Centre is located in Fife in Central Scotland. It traded from 1986–90 until finally being declared insolvent by the major investor, Scotbank plc. The owners of Glenlarch (trading as Hollyrood Hotels Ltd), were two partners with considerable experience of the hotel industry. On the basis of their reputations, feasibility study and business plan, they had obtained financial backing from a number of institutions and private investors prior to opening. The bankrupcy came as a considerable shock to all parties and the property is to be sold.

A future potential operator of this property has asked for a report to:

1. Asses the potential worth of the property.

2. Explain why the venture failed as a country house hotel and leisure centre.

Guthrie and Keppie Solicitors and Estate Agents, acting in connection with the sale of Glenlarch Country House Hotel and Leisure Centre, have provided information at your request (which includes trading and property details).

Location

The property is located in 25 acres of lightly-wooded grounds and the main buildings possess parking facilities for up to 40 cars. The nearest town is Dunblane, a popular commuter town for people employed in Glasgow or Edinburgh. Indeed, the property is well placed to benefit from the good motor and rail links to the tourist capital of Edinburgh and the cosmopolitan city of Glasgow. To the north, the towns of Dundee and Stirling offer historical interest and pleasing locations, while to the north west the highlands are also relatively close. As well as good road and rail links there are airports in Edinburgh, Glasgow and Aberdeen, offerring domestic and international connections.

History and background

The property was the former home of the Dutchess of Inverskeane who sold the property, adjoining building and surrounding land to Hollyrood Hotels in 1984 for £4.7 million. At the time of the sale, the property was not a hotel but had been used as a family home. The majority of the house is Victorian, although some parts of the house were previously a castle dating back to 1540. The house is a Grade 1 listed building considered to be of outstanding historical interest. Conversion of the house into a hotel, and subsequently a leisure club, commenced in late 1984 and alterations were completed by 1986 (for the hotel), and 1987 (for the leisure facility).

Facilities and particulars

The hotel comprises 32 bedrooms, all *en suite*, each individually decorated to designer standard. The breakdown of room type is as follows:

10 single bedrooms with private bathrooms

8 twin bedrooms with private bathrooms

8 double bedrooms with private bathrooms

6 suites.

All rooms have titles as opposed to numbers, and the emphasis was on luxury accommodation. The accommodation market was roughly split between business guests and domestic/overseas guests. Full details of accommodation rates and occupancy statistics are shown in Appendix 1.

The restaurant, which is situated in what was known as the Great Hall seats 60 persons comfortably. Function and banqueting facilities could cater for up to 75 people, and the hotel had entertained a number of small-scale, up-market conferences. The restaurant served high-quality French food, and had been aimed primarily at overnight guests and the high spending local market (see Appendix 2). Unfortunately, owing to a failure to establish a market presence in the area, and because of competition from chain-run, larger hotels benefitting from economies of scale, restaurant sales never grew to the levels predicted and declined steadily in recent years (see Appendix 3).

Adjacent to the reception is a pleasant log fire bar. The Palm Court, immediately to the rear of the reception, acts as an overspill for the bar area. The bar attracted a select local trade and seats 30 people comfortably.

The leisure centre opened some eleven months after the hotel and includes: a swimming pool, sauna, jacuzzi, solarium, fitness training centre and four squash courts. The leisure centre has a small bar attached, which served a range of alcoholic beverages. All leisure facilities were provided free for hotel guests as an improved aspect of the product, and local customers were allowed to use the facilities at a standard day rate of £5.50 for adults and £3 for children (1989 tariff). Alternatively, local clientele could join the leisure club at an annual cost of £1,450 (1989 tariff).

Initial usage of the facilities by locals was low, but after a period of months awareness of the facilities grew and consequently usage increased. External membership of the club grew quickly during the first year, but during the second and third years of trading there was a growing tendency not to renew membership (for a detailed analysis see Appendix 4). It should be noted that management did attempt to introduce a number of promotional techniques to increase leisure club membership — free membership for children aged under twelve, and discount vouchers issued for meals taken in the hotel restaurant, for example. However, such schemes failed to increase leisure centre membership significantly. In addition, the number of people who became day members was dissappointing, and it is believed that the majority of the local population made use of the large public sector facilities, which are considerably cheaper although less conveniently situated.

Hotel organisation

Organisation Chart: Glenlarch Country House Hotel and Leisure Club (as at 1990)

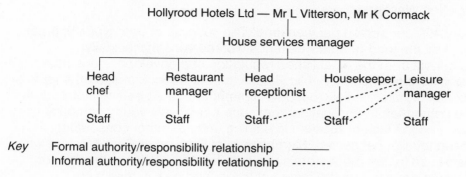

Key   Formal authority/responsibility relationship   ———

Informal authority/responsibility relationship   --------

Funding note

Funding for the project was financed by Hollyrood Hotels (41 per cent equity). The remainder of the finance came from Scotbank and a combination of bank loans, venture capital and debenture issue. The new owner will not be bound to take on any member of Hollyrood Hotels staff since all were made redundant when the company ceased trading. A full picture of trading can be found in Appendix 5.

Marketing

On the opening of the hotel, considerable effort was made to give the property both a national and an international profile. Public Relations First Consultants were hired to manage the marketing promotion and associated publicity of the opening.

A number of key sectors were identified as potential markets for the hotel in the initial feasibility plan conducted prior to the conversion. It is useful and of benefit for any interested parties to understand how the company attempted to attract such sectors and to what extent the company was successful. The short break market was identified as having considerable potential, thus two types of short breaks were developed and marketed. Low-cost weekends were developed on the following themes:

- Highland Walking Weekend
- Country Cooking Weekend
- Hunting and Shooting Weekend.

These retailed at £250 per person per weekend (arrive Friday depart Sunday), to include all meals, all activities and a gift of silver-plated hip flask with the hotel name, address and telephone number engraved upon it.

A second, more upmarket, short-break package was promoted on the following themes:

- Fine Wine Appreciation Weekend

- Gourmets and Gastronomes Weekend
- Literary Scotland — a weekend of culture and heritage
- Fine Art Appreciation Weekend.

These retailed at £450 per person per weekend. The success of both types of break was mixed, although all the food-related weekends worked very successfully.

In an attempt to benefit from the established reputation of a developed consortium, the owning company were advised by Public Relations First Consultants to attempt to join Relais & Chateaux or, alternatively, become a member of the Leading Hotels of the World. It should be noted that an application from such a relatively young company would be ambitious, and the lack of success in gaining entry to either consortium should not have been totally unexpected. Membership of Consort or Best Western was considered but dismissed by the proprietors since they felt association with either of these consortium would detract from the image of luxury and quality they were attempting to present at Glenlarch.

Special Facilities

The Glenlarch Country House Hotel and Leisure Club could cater for wheelchair bound guests. In total, some three bedrooms were converted for the use of disabled visitors, and all facilities were designed and converted with total accessibility in mind.

Appendix 1: Glenlarch Hotel — Accommodation and Occupancy Information

ACCOMMODATION OCCUPANCY (PERCENTAGE)

1987	1988	1989	1990
42%	56%	63%	62%

ROOM RATE (RACK)

	1987	1988	1989	1990
Single bedroom	£ 75	£ 80	£ 85	£ 90
Twin bedroom	£ 85	£ 90	£ 90	£ 95
Double bedroom	£ 85	£ 90	£ 90	£ 95
Suite	£115	£120	£125	£130

ACCOMMODATION REVENUE

1987	1988	1989	1990
£344,127	£485,327	£504,789	£494,501

Source: Hollyrood Hotels Ltd

Appendix 2: Glenlarch Marketing Information

CUSTOMER PROFILE, FOOD AND BEVERAGE OPERATION 1987–90

Socioeconomic profile of customers	1987 %	1988 %	1989 %	1990 %
A	10	13	15	20
B1	19	25	30	35
B2	11	17	25	25
C1	40	35	30	20
C2	20	10	–	–

Source: Public Relations First Consultants — Assignment 2; Glenlarch Feasibility Study 1985–6.

Appendix 3: Glenlarch Hotel — Restaurant Sales

RESTAURANT OCCUPANCY BY MEAL (PER CENT) AND YEAR

Meal	1987	1988	1989	1990
Breakfast	33%	49%	54%	52%
Lunch	12%	14%	13%	11%
Dinner	43%	57%	41%	37%

RESTAURANT AVERAGE SPEND (FOOD) BY MEAL AND YEAR

Meal	1987	1988	1989	1990
Breakfast	£ 7.75	£ 8.00	£ 8.25	£ 8.50
Lunch	£ 9.00	£ 9.75	£10.50	£11.25
Dinner	£15.50	£16.50	£19.50	£22.00

SALES REVENUE RESTAURANT (FOOD) BY MEAL AND YEAR

Meal	1987	1988	1989	1990
Breakfast	£ 38,018	£ 52,326	£ 60,706	£ 61,553
Lunch	£ 23,652	£ 29,893	£ 29,893	£ 27,101
Dinner	£145,963	£205,969	£175,090	£178,266

Source: Hollyrood Hotels Ltd

Appendix 4: Glenlarch Leisure Club — Financial Information

LEISURE CLUB MEMBERSHIP INCOME
(YEARLY SUBSCRIPTIONS)

	1988	1989	1990
Fees	£46,400	£66,700	£58,000
New members as a percentage of total members	100%	63.6%	80%
Renewals as a percentage of total members	0%	36.4%	20%

DAILY RATE INCOME

	1988	1989	1990
Adult	£3,410	£4,196	£3,795
Child	£ 453	£ 541	£ 505
Total	£3,863	£4,737	£4,300

PROFIT AND LOSS ACCOUNT FOR YEAR ENDING 1988

	Sports related £	Bar £		Total £
Sales	50,263	3,790		54,053
Cost of sales		1,516		1,516
Gross profit		2,274		52,537
Less				
Labour	32,500	716	33,216	
Other departmental expenses	432		432	
Undistributed operating expenses				
Administration and general			2,432	
Marketing			3,000	
Energy			7,972	
Property operation and maintenance			1,007	
Fixed charges				
Insurance			3,562	
Depreciation			5,500	
Rates			1,430	
Rental			730	
				59,281
(Loss)				(6,744)

PROFIT AND LOSS ACCOUNT FOR YEAR ENDING 1989

	Sports related £	Bar £		Total £
Sales	71,438	4,996		76,434
Cost of sales		1,848		1,848
Gross profit		3,148		74,586
Less				
Labour	36,900	1,014	37,914	
Other departmental expenses	879		879	
Undistributed operating expenses				
Administration and general			2,893	
Marketing			5,600	
Energy			8,643	
Property operation and maintenance			3,566	
Fixed charges				
Insurance			3,894	
Depreciation			5,500	
Rates			1,701	
Rental			730	
				71,320
(Loss)				(3,266)

PROFIT AND LOSS ACCOUNT FOR YEAR ENDING 1990

	Sports related £	Bar £		Total £
Sales	62,300	4,007		66,307
Cost of sales		1,430		1,430
Gross profit		2,577		64,877
Less				
Labour	34,020	826	34,846	
Other departmental expenses	739		739	
Undistributed operating expenses				
Administration and general			2,276	
Marketing			3,000	
Energy			8,221	
Property operation and maintenance			2,689	
Fixed charges				
Insurance			4,203	
Depreciation			5,500	
Rates			1,893	
Rental			730	
				64,097
Profit				780

Appendix 5: Glenlarch Country House Hotel — Financial Information

PROFIT AND LOSS ACCOUNT FOR YEAR ENDING 1987

	Food £	Beverage £	Accommodation £	Total £
Sales	207,633	62,289	344,127	614,049
Cost of sales	67,688	18,188		85,876
Gross profit	139,945	44,101	344,127	528,173
Less				
Labour (all departments)			201,877	
Salaries			67,000	
Other departmental expenses			20,877	
Undistributed operating expenses				
Administration and general			89,037	
Marketing			56,842	
Energy			18,421	
Property operation and maintenance			39,912	
Fixed charges				
Insurance			28,420	
Depreciation			61,404	
Rates			12,280	
				549,547
(Loss)				(21,374)

PROFIT AND LOSS ACCOUNT FOR YEAR ENDING 1988

	Food £	Beverage £	Accommodation £	Total £
Sales	288,188	89,338	485,327	862,853
Cost of sales	96,543	27,695		124,238
Gross profit	191,645	61,643	485,327	738,615
Less				
Labour (all departments)			241,598	
Salaries			68,500	
Other departmental expenses			26,748	
Undistributed operating expenses				
Administration and general			88,873	
Marketing			56,085	
Energy			24,159	
Property operation and maintenance			51,770	
Fixed charges				
Insurance			41,416	
Depreciation			86,285	
Rates			15,531	
				700,965
Profit				37,650

PROFIT AND LOSS ACCOUNT FOR YEAR ENDING 1989

	Food £	Beverage £	Accommodation £	Total £
Sales	265,689	77,049	504,789	847,527
Cost of sales	87,677	24,655		112,332
Gross profit	178,012	52,394	504,789	735,195
Less				
Labour (all departments)			233,069	
Salaries			80,500	
Other departmental expenses			27,120	
Undistributed operating expenses				
Administration and general			68,649	
Marketing			72,039	
Energy			27,120	
Property operation and maintenance			66,954	
Fixed charges				
Insurance			41,528	
Depreciation			84,752	
Rates			16,103	
				717,834
Profit				17,361

PROFIT AND LOSS ACCOUNT FOR YEAR ENDING 1990

	Food £	Beverage £	Accommodation £	Total £
Sales	266,920	68,064	494,501	829,485
Cost of sales	94,756	22,120		116,876
Gross profit	172,164	45,944	494,501	712,609
Less				
Labour (all departments)			240,550	
Salaries			82,500	
Other departmental expenses			31,520	
Undistributed operating expenses				
Administration and general			69,676	
Marketing			90,413	
Energy			34,008	
Property operation and maintenance			29,031	
Fixed charges				
Insurance			39,815	
Depreciation			82,948	
Rates			16,589	
				717,050
(Loss)				(4,441)

— 8 —

Gower Beers

Introduction

The board of directors at Gower Beers is considering the purchase of the Grand Hotel. The board is still undecided because of the somewhat run-down state of the operation. A report is required which reviews the operational possibilities of the hotel. The report must establish:

1. The growth potential of the hotel compared with the current performance and an estimate of the capital payback period.

2. Redevelopment options for the hotel.

3. An outline of (operational) budgeting policy for the hotel.

The company

Gower Beers is a medium-sized regional brewing company. During the 1960s, increasing profitability allowed the purchase of over 90 public houses (20 per cent managed, 80 per cent tenanted). This was seen as an ideal opportunity to acquire retail outlets in order to further increase beer production and, at the same time, secure stable demand. All the pubs were highly branded and sold exclusively Gower ales and, later, lager. During the 1970s and early 1980s, Gower further increased outlets by over 40 per cent, and acquired a wine and spirit distributing division.

A year ago, the company decided to develop hotel interests. The Annual Report suggested the reasons for this were diversification, prestige and anticipated profit from room sales. Gower management had observed several brewers develop hotel divisions over a number of years, but it was only when a number of close rivals started making major acquisitions that the decision to expand was made. The aim was to acquire a portfolio of five to ten medium-sized city centre hotels to extend the company brand image and, where possible, the retailing of Gower products. It was anticipated that, in contrast to the public house estate, the hotels would be company managed. The first hotel was viewed as a pilot for the development and, when finances allowed, would form the basis for the growth of a strong regional presence in the secondary hotel sector. To this end, the company had undertaken several feasibility studies in major cities in the South East and East Midlands.

Finally, the company has purchased the three-star Grand Hotel in the city of Camchester. There are hotels on the market at other locations, but the price of each is prohibitive. The hotel was owned previously by a larger brewing company that is currently divesting its interests in hotels. However, when the hotel came on the market several national hotel chains showed interest.

The hotel

Built as a three-storey, city-centre hotel during the late 1960s, the Grand Hotel has undergone some modernisation to comply with legal requirements, but requires work to bring it up to the standard of its major competitors. The bedrooms are all of adequate proportions and are currently divided into the following categories:

29 single rooms with private bathrooms

26 double rooms with private bathrooms

35 twin rooms with private bathrooms and shower

4 suites with annex and private bathrooms.

The hotel is currently rated three star, but has potential for development into four-star classification.

The hotel restaurant can seat 95. A full or continental breakfast are available to residents, and a single table d'hote lunch and dinner menu is offered to residents and passing trade. Business in the restaurant has not been good over the past year. The previous manager blamed this on competition from other hotels. In an attempt to increase sales, prices were reduced by 10 per cent. The lunch/dinner menu and wine list are shown in Appendix 3. The extensive lobby of the hotel is also used to serve tea, coffee, sandwiches and assorted pastries to customers who wish to have a quick snack. Business is brisk in the lobby but most of the guest complaints about the quality of service and the temperature of food arise from this operation. The ground floor of the hotel has several nonoperational storage areas, one is of a substantial size. The previous owners of the hotel had considered turning this area into a 50 cover themed restaurant.

The Stag Bar is used mainly by residents. Twice a week, a folk band plays in the bar and this attracks local people. It appears that most locals drink at one of the least expensive pubs in the town, or in one of the similarly priced, but more congenial, competitor hotels. The capacity of the Stag Bar is 180.

As part of the purchase, Gower Beers have agreed to retain several key members of staff, including the assistant manager, the front office manager and the head barman. However, several other key personnel, on hearing of the impending change of ownership, have already left to work in other hotels in the city. This includes the general manager, who has been employed at the Park Lodge Hotel, and the financial controller, who has been employed at the Victoria Hotel. Several long-serving supervisory staff have also left to work elsewhere.

Gower Beers intend to keep the hotel open while certain refurbishment work is undertaken, albeit at reduced capacity and discount rates. A new general manager has been recruited and the period of refurbishment should give him time to adapt to the running of the hotel.

The location

Camchester has a long history. Several ancient battles have been fought nearby, and the abbey was partly destroyed in the Middle Ages and subsequently rebuilt. The racecourse and two nationally-known stately homes situated nearby attract a large number of visitors. Camchester is the largest city in Cambridgeshire with a population of over 75,000. The local university and college students swell the local population by 11,000 each October. Several major roads, including the M11 and A1, pass through or nearby the town. The country has become a popular recreational destination because of its ease of access, its history and its pleasant environment. Approximate distances from other major cities are as follows:

Norwich	40 miles
Birmingham	70 miles
London	65 miles

The majority of the adult population is employed by a variety of service industries and agriculture. Some light industry exists, but it is located on a number of industrial estates on the outskirts of the city. Recently, a national insurance company relocated its offices to Camchester, and there has been a large influx of London commuters over the past five years. A marketing survey in 1989 classified the local adult population as follows:

Professional and managerial	17%
Other skilled white collar	23%
Skilled manual	21%
Unskilled	16%
Unemployed	6%
Retired with private pension	7%
Retired on state pension only	10%
	100%

(Source: Hospmark 1989)

There are numerous social clubs in Camchester including a young farmers' association, two shooting clubs, three riding clubs, a boating association, three bridge clubs, a rugby club, three football clubs and a cricket club.

The competition

There are thirteen hotels in Camchester, including the Grand Hotel, that have more than 20 rooms:

Hotel	Rooms	Ownership	Classification	Single Rate £
Moncrieff Arms	20	Private*	Unclassified	19.50**
Mayville Castle	20	Private	Unclassified	23.00**
Craig Hotel	23	Private*	Unclassified	17.00
Cross Keys Inn	27	Brewery owned	2 star	19.50
Fens Hotel	40	Brewery owned	2 star	23.50
Victoria Hotel	44	Private*	2 star	26.00**
Marina Hotel	50	Hotel group	Unclassified	29.00**
Park Lodge Hotel	67	Hotel group*	3 star	32.50
Kings Manor	67	Hotel group*	3 star	41.75**
Camchester Court Hotel	72	Hotel group	3 star	33.95
Raeburn House Hotel	74	Hotel group	3 star	39.00
Country Hotel	102	Hotel group	3 star	44.90**

* Member of a marketing consortium
** Includes continental breakfast

Inns, guesthouses, and bed and breakfast accommodation brings the total rooms available in the town to just over 950. The Camchester Court Hotel and the Raeburn House Hotel have the only large function suites in the city and, between them, account for almost all of the available banqueting business. However, the Victoria Hotel has recently been granted permission by the local council to erect a ground floor extension. The Park Lodge Hotel has recently undergone refurbishment, and has the only hotel health club in the city. There are two gyms nearby, but these are somewhat dated and have few leisure facilities. The main golf course in Camchester is run by the company which owns the Country Hotel. The course is conveniently situated within five minutes walk of the Country Hotel. There are five small private golf courses in and around the city. The five largest competitor hotels have high-quality restaurants and, together with three independent 'free-standing' restaurants, account for most of the tourist lunch and dinner trade. Other dining facilities comprise two Indian restaurants, three Chinese restaurants, a kebab house, a coffee shop, three fish and chip shops, three company-owned pizza restaurants and a burger restaurant.

There are over 30 public houses in the city, 75 per cent of which are brewery owned — Gower Beers owns four of them. Tourists and other visitors to the city tend to use the hotel bars, which have a range of themes including cocktail bar, wine bar and traditional lounge bar styling.

The market

Over the past decade, Camchester's tourist trade has grown considerably — its history, architectural heritage and pleasant surrounding countryside all make it an attractive place to visit. In recent years, activity sports holidays have grown in popularity and several operators have set up in the city to cater for activities such as equestrian events, shooting and other field sports, hill walking and fishing.

Examples of the tour agencies currently operating in Camchester are:

• MacPhee Field Sporting Holidays is a specialist tour operator who established an office in Camchester in 1988. It arranges sporting breaks including transport, accommodation and tours for clients from all over the UK.

- Anglia Angling is a fishing school catering for all levels of anglers. It provides accommodation, tuition and fishing passes for many of the best rivers in the area.

- Moving Target Ltd specialises in providing residential shooting trips to corporate executives.

- Equine Sports Ltd is a residential riding school that offers packages from three to seven days.

The number of domestic tourists visiting the area is difficult to estimate, as few surveys specifically about the city have been conducted. However, a recent tourist authority survey of hotels and tourist attractions in the country as a whole indicated that business was good and increasing, particularly at the two extremes of customer spend. The total number of domestic visits to the country in 1989 were 2,900,500. The same survey also noted that nonbusiness visitors to Camchester arrive predominantly by car and in groups of two to four, and the average length of stay is 2.6 days per visitor. It also highlighted that 70 per cent of visitors were within 1.5 hours' driving time.

The overseas tourist market to the city tends to be volatile. For example, in 1987 the number of American visitors fell and many hotels were left with low occupancy during the peak season because of cancellations. However, of those tourists that did visit the city last year (1989), 42 per cent came from the USA, 34 per cent came from Western Europe and 15 per cent came from Japan. Local traders expect growth in the number of visitors from Europe after 1992. The tourist authority survey indicated that 445,000 overseas visited the country in 1989.

Appendix 1: The Grand Hotel — Financial Information

1. SUMMARY OF INFORMATION FROM TRADING AND PROFIT AND LOSS ACCOUNT FOR PERIOD 1 JANUARY TO 31 DECEMBER 1989

	Rooms £	Food £	Beverage £	Total £
Sales	357,930	340,427	174,533	872,890
Cost of sales	–	139,575	75,057	214,632
Labour costs				
Departmental	82,314	54,468	24,435	161,217
General Salaries				69,831
Other departmental operating expenses	46,525	20,426	15,710	82,661
Undistributed operating expenses				
Administration and general				29,831
Marketing				13,093
Energy				52,373
Property operation and maintenance				43,645
Fixed charges				152,756
Profit before tax				52,851

2. SALES, GROSS PROFIT AND NET PROFIT 1983–8

	1983 £	1984 £	1985 £	1986 £	1987 £	1988 £
Sales	534,200	578,340	745,050	737,950	703,700	716,875
Gross profit	443,000	456,200	532,675	552,725	489,775	494,644
Net profit	85,475	86,754	81,956	83,388	64,740	58,067

3. 1989 TARIFFS

£49.00 per person per night including VAT only (April to September)
£41.50 per person per night including VAT only (October to March)

4. HOTEL BED OCCUPANCY FOR 1988 AND 1989

Year	Jan	Feb	Mar	Apr	May	Jun	Jul	Aug	Sep	Oct	Nov	Dec
1989	9%	5%	25%	49%	69%	72%	94%	92%	70%	50%	31%	4%
1990	10%	11%	13%	40%	51%	62%	63%	71%	51%	47%	32%	17%

Appendix 2: The Grand Hotel — Current Refurbishment Cost (estimates) 1990

General exterior building work	£65,000
General internal work (back of house)	£142,000
Refurbishment one room	£6,400
Redecoration of Stag Bar	£45,000
Redecoration of restaurant	£42,000
Refurbishment of front of house and public areas	£29,700
New plant and equipment required	£47,000*
General building work (car park)	£17,400

*Note: This includes front office microcomputers, EPOS system and new kitchen equipment.

Appendix 3: The Grand Hotel — Menu and Wine List

Restaurant Table d'Hote Menu

Fixed Price £13.50

Freshly made Soup of the Day served with Crusty Roll and Butter

or

Potted Shrimp served with Mayonnaise and Brown Bread Fingers

or

Finely sliced, Spiced Smoked Ham served with Cucumber and Dill Sauce

or

A choice of Fresh Fruit Juice

———

Paupiettes of Lemon Sole served with a Prawn and Crab Sauce

or

Roast Sirloin of Beef in a Red Wine and Mushroom Sauce

or

Half a Baby Roast Chicken served with Salad

or

Roast Lamb Stuffed with Walnuts and Rosemary

or

Vegetarian Crepe stuffed with Broccoli and covered in Smoked Cheese Sauce

———

Orange Bavarios served with Pineapple

or

Fresh Fruit Salad

or

Selection of Gateaux

———

Tea or Coffee with mints

———

*Main dishes are served with a choice of potatoes (roast, saute or creamed)
and fresh seasonal vegetables.*

Restaurant Wine List

Red Wines

France	(Bottle price)
Chateau de Boisett, Bordeaux Rouge (1987)	£ 6.90
Chateau Le Cadet, Bordeaux Superieur (1980)	£14.50
Beaujolais-Villages	£ 7.90
Cotes du Rhone, Domaine St Apollinaire (1987)	£ 8.45
Vin de Pays de L'Aude (House Wine)	£ 6.60
House Wine by the glass	£ 1.40

Italy	
Chianti Classico	£ 8.85
Bardolino	£ 6.90

Spain	
Rioja, Marques de Laceres (1982)	£ 9.70

Other Red Wines	
Australian Shiraz-Cabernet, (1986)	£ 7.30
Chilean Cabernet Sauvignon	£ 7.10
Yugoslavian Merlot	£ 6.75

White Wines

France	(Bottle price)
Chateau de Boissante, Entre-Deux-Mers (1987)	£ 6.95
Macon Villages La Foret (1986/87)	£ 9.90
Muscadet de Serve et Maine Sur Lie	£ 7.35
Cotes du Rhone Blanc	£ 6.90
Vin de Pays des Cotes du Tarn (House Wine)	£ 6.50
House Wine by the glass	£ 1.35

Italy	
Lambrusco Bianco	£ 6.20
Arebbiano di Romagna	£ 8.70
Frascati Secco	£ 8.95

Germany	
Berich Nierstein, Rheinhessen	£ 7.70
Liebfraumilch	£ 6.85
Deutscher Tafelwein	£ 6.85
Bereich Bernkastel	£ 6.95

Other White Wines	
Australian Reisling, Barossa Valley	£ 8.10

Rose and Sparkling Wines

Anjou Rose	£ 7.30
Montlouis Mousseux	£ 9.90
House Champagne, Jacques Perrier et Fils	£13.00

— 9 —

Gladwell Civic Centre

As sales executive for Gladwell Civic Centre Ltd you are required by the company to produce a tender document for the catering concession at the Gladwell Civic Centre.
   The tender document must include the following information:

1. A statement of the overall catering policy to be adopted.

2. An outline of operating procedures.

3. A financial summary.

Introduction

The Gladwell Civic Centre has long been a busy community facility. The total number of people who visited the centre last year (1989) is shown in Appendix 1. In 1990, the number of visitors is expected to increase because of the festival of culture that is due to take place in the city throughout that year.
   In the building is a cafeteria which has proved to be very popular with local residents. However, a growth in the number of 'special' civic functions has led the administrators to review the operation of the catering facility. After an initial investigation, it became apparent that the existing provision was inadequate to cope with the increase in specialist catering, and that a contractor would be considered to take over the catering operation. A tender notice was prepared by the administration committee.

The Tender notice

NOTICE OF TENDER

Tenders for the catering concession are required for the catering provision at the Gladwell Civic Centre as of 1 September 1990.

The Tender will be issued to the most appropriate contractor for an initial period of two years, with the option to renew each subsequent year by mutual agreement between the contractor and the centre administration. It is the intention of the administration to monitor the quality of the catering provision on a regular basis by independent inspector. If, at any time, the independent inspector has cause to report a sub-standard catering provision, then the administration reserves the right to investigate the situation and, if necessary, withdraw the concession by giving 90 days notice. If at any time the contractor wishes to withdraw from the concession, the same notice period of 90 days shall be required in writing.

Tenders to be submitted in writing by 31 May 1990 to:

The Administrator of Public Services,
The Civic Centre, Gladwell, GL1 1AB

Opening times of the centre

The Civic Centre is open to the public from 10 am to 5 pm Monday to Saturday, and from 12 noon to 4 pm on Sunday. It is closed on certain bank holidays and other holidays. In total, the centre is open for 355 days per year and the catering facilities will be available on the same basis. General catering facilities will be offered from 11 am to 4 pm Monday to Friday, and from 12.30 pm to 3 pm on Sundays. In addition, special lunch and evening functions will be provided by the contractor upon request.

General catering requirements

The administration wishes to develop the catering facility into an efficient catering outlet that covers all its direct expenses, contributes funds to the general administration of the building, and requires only contractor staffing.

The Civic Centre is situated in the heart of the city (population 1,500,000), and is within five minutes walking distance of the main shopping precinct. The close proximity of university and college buildings means that many of the visitors to the cafeteria are students. The existing facility, although basic, is popular with the students because it is one of the least expensive places in the area to buy coffee and snacks.

It is intended that a single menu offering beverages, snacks and main meals would be offered throughout the time the cafeteria is open. While not attempting to mimic the commercial catering operations in the area, the administration intends to compete with them for business.

Initially, special function menus would be for civic receptions, conferences and seminars. However, it is intended that the contractor should market the facility for private functions outside usual hours. Prices for such functions should be competitive and a proportion of the profit will be given to the centre. The contractor will not be required to pay for the fixed charges of the catering operation. A minimum fee of £15,000 will be paid by the contractor for the concession in the first year, and £16,200 in the second. After the second year, the contract will be renegotiated. All direct operating expenses (including energy expenses which are monitored by meter), will be paid by the contractor.

The catering facility

A general plan of the cafeterial and preparation area appears in Appendix 2. The cafeteria can be entered from either the street or through the ground floor of the building. The customer area currently seats 35 people, but this could be increased to approximately 50 by more effective positioning of furniture. The kitchen and preparation areas are small but adequate, and most equipment is relatively new. The servery area has always been a problem — at most lunchtimes a queue forms which spills out the door and into the main lobby. The administrators have insisted that the new facility must overcome this problem, and have allocated funds should the servery counter require modernisation.

Special functions should take place in a large hall adjacent to the lobby. This can cater for approximately 100 guests at a reception or finger buffet, and for 60 for a seated dinner. The hall is conveniently situated opposite the kitchen on the main ground floor area, and can be accessed by the caterers from a service corridor. The quality of decor in the hall is very high, and is equal to many of the best traditional hotels in the city.

A summary of 1989 Trading Results for the centre is included in Appendix 3.

Preliminary menus have already been produced by Caterwell with relevant cost information and provisional sales estimates. These are presented in Appendix 4 and show general menu items and function menus classified according to cost. It is anticipated that the final menus may differ in detail, but that the cost structure for them will remain the same. The sales estimates may require revision at a later date, but for the moment are being used for budgeting purposes.

Appendix 1: Gladwell Civic Centre — Visitors (1989)

Visitors

General public	255,500
OAPS	11,400
Educational visits	22,345
Other	96,780
Total	386,025

Special Function Catering

Lunch reception	1,080
Evening receptions	1,790
Dinners	220
Total	3,090

Appendix 2: Gladwell Civic Centre — Plan of Catering Facilities

Appendix 3: Gladwell Civic Centre — Cafeteria Trading Summary 1989

Sales Information

Cafeteria sales	£59,300
Gross profit	£39,500
Other direct expenses	£17,325
Contribution to funds	£ 2,475
Function sales	£16,840
Gross profit	£10,945
Other direct expenses	£ 4,400
Contribution to funds	£ 1,475

Appendix 4: Gladwell Civic Centre — Expenses and Sales Estimates

Produced by Caterwell Industrial Caterers Ltd, December 1989

CAFETERIA MENU
(GROSS PROFIT PERCENTAGES ARE TARGETS FOR PRICING PURPOSES)

Food item	Average portion cost £	Anticipated weekly sales
Starters (gross profit 55%)		
Vegetable soups	0.34	20
Cream/meat soups	0.42	15
Various salads (small)	0.24	10
Other cold starters	0.40	10
Hot snacks (gross profit 57%)		
Various pies	0.21	10
Pizza slice	0.22	10
Croissant with filling	0.31	5
Baked potato with filling	0.22	15
Toasted sandwich	0.35	5
Cold snacks (gross profit 57%)		
Sandwiches	0.21	25
Filled rolls	0.19	20
Various salads (medium)	0.32	5
Various quiches	0.37	10
Pâté with French bread	0.38	5

Food item	Average portion cost £	Anticipated weekly sales
Hot main dishes (gross profit 55%)		
Beef dish of the day	0.60	15
Chicken dish of the day	0.53	15
Fish dish of the day	0.54	5
Pasta dish of the day	0.48	5
Vegetarian dish of the day	0.48	30
Hot flans	0.39	20
Cold main dishes (gross profit 60%)		
Various salads (large)	0.42	5
Ploughman's lunch	0.47	5
Main dish accompaniments (gross profit 53%)		
Vegetables of the day	0.19	40
Portion of french fries	0.16	35
Various side salads	0.24	5
Desserts and Pastries (gross profit 58%)		
Hot desserts	0.33	10
Cold desserts	0.29	5
Various ices	0.17	20
Pastries	0.24	20
Beverages (gross profit 72%)		
Coffee	0.12	420
Tea	0.10	350
Milk	0.12	35
Beverages (gross profit 60%)		
Carbonated drinks	0.17	150
Mineral water	0.22	40
Non-alcohol wine (white)	0.34	5
Low-alcohol lager	0.38	10

SPECIALITY FUNCTION MENUS (TO BE PRICED AT A GROSS PROFIT OF 65 PER CENT)
RECEPTION AND BUFFET MENUS ARE AVAILABLE AT LUNCH OR IN THE EVENING

Food item	Average portion cost £	Anticipated monthly sales
Drinks reception	1.58	2 × 20
Finger buffet	1.67	1 × 50
Various Quiches		
Bouchees		
Sausage Rolls		
Various Sandwiches		
Canapes		

Food item	Average portion cost £	Anticipated monthly sales
Cold Buffet (A) Florida Cocktail	1.84	2 × 40
Cold Roast Meats Salad Selection		
Creme Caramel		
Cold Buffet (B) Asparagus Quiche or Salmon Mousse	2.64	1 × 40
Chicken Drumsticks Roast Spiced Beef Vegetarian Vol-Au-Vents Salad Selection		
Bakewell Tart or Fruit Salad		
Coffee or Tea		
Hot Buffet (A) Scotch Broth	2.10	1 × 40
Goujons of Sole Roast Rib of Beef Vegetable Selection		
Rum Baba with Cream		
Hot Buffet (B) Consumé Juliene or Stuffed Tomato	2.81	2 × 40
Chicken Maryland Beef Olives Roast Lamb with Mint Vegetable Selection		
Apple Tart with Cream or Orange Bavarios		
Coffee or Tea		
Three Course Dinner (A) Potage Bonne Femme	3.18	1 × 30
Contrefilet de Boeuf Roti		

Food item	Average portion cost £	Anticipated monthly sales
ou Omelette aux Fines Herbs Legumes et Pommes Persilees		
Peche Cardinal ou Coupe Jamaique		
Café ou The		
Three Course Dinner (B) Melon Frappe ou Salad au poire et Noix	3.48	2 × 30
Colettes d'Agneau Vert Pre ou Escalope de Porc Holstein ou Contrefilet de Boeuf Roti		
Pommes Rotis ou Pommes Anna Mais au Beurre, Chouxfleur Polonaise, Carottes a la Creme		
Bavarois a L'Orange ou Tarte au Normande		
Café ou The		
Four Course Dinner Coupe de Pamplemousse Frappe ou Mousse de Saumon	3.78	1 × 15
Gratin aux Fruits de Mer ou Filet de Sole Veronique		
Supreme de Volaille Richelieu ou Coute d'Agneau Garno ou Filet de Boeuf Stroganoff		
Pommes Rotis ou Pommes Marquise, Mais au Beurre, Choux de Bruxelles aux Marrons, Carottes Vichy		
Café ou The et Petit Four		

ESTIMATES OF OTHER DIRECT COSTS

Labour: catering managers salary	£ 8,750
All other labour costs	11% of sales revenue
Other expenses	9% of sales revenue

— 10 —

Riverland Bar-Restaurants plc

Riverland Bar–Restaurants plc is a chain of fifteen themed bar-restaurants located in the Midlands and Derbyshire. The restaurant chain was previously owned by a brewing company, but some two years ago the properties were sold in one lot to a partnership. The restaurant's have a standard theme: they benefit from a uniform management structure; and a management incentive scheme is in operation. Operational performance over the past two years has been stable in both food and liquor sales, although costs in certain areas have started to behave in a somewhat erratic manner in the majority of units.

As performance is causing the proprietors some concern, your company, Performance Review Consulting Services, have been requested to analyse current performance and propse an action plan for the improvement of profit and sales. As the consultant, you must provide a report for the proprietors. Your report should be no longer than 1,500 words (exclusive of appendicies), and an executive summary should be contained at the commencement of the report.

The following information has been provided and should help in the production of your response.

Ownership and structure of Riverland Bar–Restaurants plc

In May 1988 the ownership of the group changed. Previously, the restaurant chain had been part of the catering and leisure division of Parker and Cole, a regional brewery. The brewery company made a long-term decision to move out of catering and leisure. Thus in May 1988 the fifteen restaurants were purchased by Mr K Kiernon (of Kiernon & Co Construction) and Mr R Tomlinson (of R T Building Services Contractors). The partners have equal shares in the company and decided to buy the chain in an effort to diversify their business interests, moving into sectors outside the building and construction work trade.

The partners, who have no previous experience of the catering industry, were content to retain the organisational structure and a number of senior staff that they inherited in the takeover from Parker and Cole. Fifteen units throughout the company correspond to the typical unit management structure illustrated.

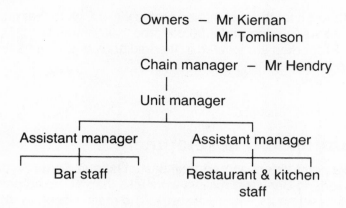

Owners – Mr Kiernan
Mr Tomlinson

Chain manager – Mr Hendry

Unit manager

Assistant manager   Assistant manager

Bar staff   Restaurant & kitchen
staff

Organisation

The proprietors take little interest in the operational aspects of the business and are quite content for the chain manager, Mr Hendry, to take full control of the management of the group. At the end of each month, Mr Hendry provides a unit report summary for the owners and a discussion of that month's operations takes place. Mr Hendry sees his job as essentially one of keeping sales and profitability in line with budget. All managers have, since 1988, participated in the management incentive scheme, which allows managers to earn large bonuses if they achieve budgeted targets. This has led to good management retention rates.

Each unit manager is allowed to run his/her unit, arrange suppliers, printing, laundry, staffing, and training with little interference from Mr Hendry — as long as profitability and sales levels are on target. Mr Hendry prefers to recruit managers from within the group rather than advertise externally. Within the units operational staff are recruited locally through job centres, local newspaper advertisements and through contact with local catering colleges.

Size and style of operation

Each unit seats approximately 100 in the restaurant and a further 50 in the bar area. The decoration is standard and takes the theme of river sports and the southern states of America. This is reflected in the menu, decor, props and waiters' outfits. The menu is standard, and a copy is included in Appendix 1. Menus are 'revised' annually although, in truth, they do not change radically — the theme is established, popular and requires little revision.

All units have taken advantage of the relaxed licensing hours and, since March 1989, all units have remained open for food and liquor from noon to 11 pm each day. The full menu is served throughout the day, although it is still the case that the majority of business occurs between noon and 2.00 pm, and 7.00 pm and 10.30 pm, for both food and liquor sales. Properties are located in the Midlands and Derbyshire. Locations are detailed in Appendix 2.

Labour, training and development

The units rely to a great extent on part-time casual labour. Some 66 per cent of all employees of Riverland Bar–Restaurants work less than 16 hours per week. A further 20 per cent work less than 24 hours per week. The main reason for this is that such employees are flexible in the hours they work and are 'on call' during busy periods. A summary of labour information is included in Appendix 3. Supervisory staff are all scheduled to work 39 hours per week although this is rarely the case and the real average is nearer to 55 hours. Assistant managers and managers are both paid a fixed monthly salary, which is not related to hours worked. Unit managers do, however, qualify for bonuses based on the achievement of sales levels.

All personnel matters, such as training, development and staffing at unit level, are left to the individual unit managers, who are interviewed and appointed by the chain manager, Mr Hendry. Labour turnover, absenteeism and sickness are recognised problems, but are considered acceptable if profit levels are maintained. Full financial results for the group during 1988–9 are presented in Appendix 4.

A problem that is acknowledged is the quality of service, and management have been involved in a central training initiative sponsored by the proprietors to try and improve service and the meal experience guests recieve. At unit level, staff are encouraged to compete against each other to receive 'care awards'.

The results to date have not been encouraging. Unit management report that the enthusiasm of staff is not great because of the low level of total reward involved. What is more, the promotional material and money vouchers used in the scheme were viewed as uninspiring.

Other major training initiatives within the company are centred on the formal, systematic training programmes of the Hotel and Catering Training Board. Each unit manager is in possession of 'on job' training certificates TS1 and TS2. It is a company policy that all unit managers should be trained to TS3 by December 1991, and all assistant managers to TS2 by March 1992.

The development pattern of staff is not consistent throughout the company. At some units, managers and assistant managers have been recruited and promoted from within the company, although at the majority of units it has become necessary to advertise locally for managerial and supervisory staff. However, the prohibitive costs of such an exercise are seen as unacceptable by Mr Hendry, and a contributing factor to the low net profit recorded in March 1990.

Sales and marketing

Sales and marketing is handled both centrally and at unit level. Mr Hendry has overall control of the marketing budget. The recorded over spend in the most recent figures provided will be compensated for by a reduction in spending in next year's budget.

Summary of Marketing Expenditure

	£
Budget marketing expenditure (1989–90)	450,000
Actual marketing expenditure (1989–90)	461,041
Overspend	11,041
Carry forward to next year's budgeted figures	
Budgeted marketing expenditure (1990–1)	472,500
Less overspend (1989–90)	11,041
Revised budgeted marketing expenditure (1990–1)	461,459

The market budget is allocated in the following way:

Head office advertising	35%
Head office sponsored internal promotions	5%
Allocated to units in proportion to their sales levels	60%
Total marketing expenses	100%

Such budgeting fits the group philosophy of minimal head office control over unit management, so long as profitability is maintained. Unit managers are thus responsible for their own marketing budget although they must produce, where possible, receipts to prove expenditure in this area.

Company development and expansion

The company believes that its product is now tried and tested and Mr Hendry is currently considering expansion in a northerly direction. Southern expansion is seen as unwise since branded eating 'competition' is already well established there. Competitors in the south of England benefit from an established market presence and can draw upon economies of scale that large organisations enjoy for a variety of needs ranging from printing to purchasing foodstuffs.

Six cities have been targeted for a 40 per cent expansion of the company:

Aberdeen
Carlisle
Edinburgh
Glasgow
Newcastle-upon-Tyne
York

It is the intention of the company to purchase freehold city centre properties in established or developing locations. Conversions of older buildings, making use of local grand aid and European funding, are being considered actively by Mr Hendry and the proprietors. This will further expand the tangible assets of the company and allow Riverland Bar–Restaurants to establish itself as a nationwide operator in the branded eating market.

Funding for expansion will come directly from net profits and loan capital. The proprietors do not intend to fund more than 10 per cent of the cost of expansion from their noncatering interests. At present, Mr Hendry is in consultation with three finance companies with a view to funding expansion plans. The current company gearing ratio is 1:04, or 40 per cent.

Appendix 1: Riverland Bar–Restaurants — Menu

Old Southern Starters

SEAFOOD CREOLE   £3.99

Flaked smoked salmon, prawns and seafood laced with spicy mayonnaise and served with tortilla corn chips.

MISSISSIPPI SEAFOOD COCKTAIL   £3.99

Cold water prawns with a perky seafood dressing on a bed of lettuce combined with other seafood favourites served with hot brown roll and butter.

MELON BOAT 'LOUISIANA'   £2.15

A generous slice of fresh melon decorated with a slice of orange and ginger, sugar to taste.

UNCLE TOMS POTATO SKINS   £2.99

A starter with a difference based on old recipes – this provides a real taste of the Deep South; potato skins with mixed vegetables deep fried and served with sour cream dressing.

GUACAMOLE   £2.50

A delicate blend of puréed avocado, creamy mayonnaise and tabasco. Served with a selection of fresh crudités and hot toasted pitta bread.

OLD SOUTH CHOWDER   £3.25

A traditional favourite, a thick warming seafood chowder served with hot wholemeal bread.

SOUTH CAROLINA SUCCOTASH   £3.00

A healthy taste of the Old South with a variety of lima beans and vegetables with a hint of chilli to warm up most appetites.

CAROLINA CRUDITIES   £2.50

A host of fresh vegetable cruditiés, served on crushed ice for you to taste and enjoy with our three sauce dip. There's spicy seafood dip, sour cream succotash and ritzy tomato.

Riverland Bar–Restaurants

Main Courses

All main courses include in their price:

 * New potatoes, or french fried potatoes, or freshly baked jacket potato served with your choice of sour cream and chives or butter

 * South Carolina Succotash and Herb Bread served warm from our ovens

SOUTHERN PORK SURPRISE £5.10

Two tender pork loin steaks served with a creamy apple, beer and brandy sauce.

HALF A ROASTED CHICKEN £5.65

Mouthwatering roast chicken served with our superb savoury barbeque sauce.

8oz GAMMON STEAK 'MISSISSIPPI' £6.15

A juicy gammon steak topped with your choice of fried egg or tangy pineapple and orange.

OLD AUNTY SADIE'S HALF A ROASTED DUCK £7.95

A rich succulent duck served with a traditional tangy orange sauce from Aunty Sadie's original recipe.

CONFEDERATE STATES SEAFOOD PLATTER £6.40

A delicious combination of scampi. scallops, plaice and haddock deep fried to a golden brown.

VEGEBEAN CHILLI £4.90

A spicy mixture of tomatoes red kidney beans, lima beans cracked wheat, peppers and walnuts. Served with a fresh pasta salad and tortilla chips.

BEEF AND BEAN STIR FRY £7.90

A combination of spicy beef and various beans served with wild 'black rice' for a tangy and different experience.

10 oz STEAK DIANE MISSISSIPPI £9.95

A classic cut of prime beef served with mushrooms, brandy and cream.

12 oz PRIME SOUTHERN SIRLOIN 'CAJUN' £10.95

A large prime sirloin grilled to your liking served with traditional Cajun accompaniements.

18 oz PRIME RUMP STEAK 'PEPPER-MOMA' £12.75

Over a pound of rump steak for the large appetite of the old south served with a brandy based sauce with crushed peppercorns and cream.

Riverland Bar–Restaurants

DESSERTS

SOUTH CAROLINA CHOCOLATE AND ORANGE SUNDAE	£3.25	FANTASY FAYRE	£2.50
		OLD SOUTH SHERRY TRIFLE	£3.00
COFFEE CREAM TORTE	£2.95	FRESH FRUIT SOUTHERN 'BELLE'	£2.00
STRAWBERRIES, ICE CREAM	£3.00		
and southern style cracker biscuit nest. Try it!		RASPBERRY PAVLOVA	£2.50
CHOCOLATE 'BOMB' SURPRISE	£3.50	THE CHEESBOARD	£2.50
Robert E Lee's Revenge			

'OLD SOUTH' RIVERLAND
CUSTOMER SATISFACTION GUARANTEE

Everything about your meal should be entirely to your satifaction.

If it is not please tell your waiter or waitress at the time so that it can be put right for you.

If you are not satisfied get the manager out!!

A service charge of 10% is levied. All further graduities are at the discretion of the customer.
All our prices include VAT.

Appendix 2: Riverland Bar–Restaurants — Location of Properties

Key

- Existing restaurant location
- ○ Proposed restaurant expansion

Appendix 3: Riverland Bar–Restaurants — Summary of Labour Information

OPERATING INFORMATION

	1987	1988	1989
Absenteeism — days lost	6.7%	8.3%	12.7%
Sickness — days lost	5.1%	5.9%	7.9%
Labour turnover (not including management)	29	37	49
Labour turnover at supervision unit level	12	18	39
Labour turnover at management unit level	10	0	0

Appendix 4: Riverland Bar–Restaurants — Financial Information

YEAR ENDING 1989 UNIT RESULTS

		£
Unit 1	Sales	845,300
	Gross profit food and beverages	583,257
	Net profit	101,436
Unit 2	Sales	650,030
	Gross profit food and beverages	386,768
	Net profit	68,223
Unit 3	Sales	497,580
	Gross profit food and beverages	313,475
	Net profit	57,222
Unit 4	Sales	594,550
	Gross profit food and beverages	368,621
	Net profit	74,318
Unit 5	Sales	736,000
	Gross profit food and beverages	478,400
	Net profit	101,200
Unit 6	Sales	749,900
	Gross profit food and beverages	502,433
	Net profit	80,614
Unit 7	Sales	524,000
	Gross profit food and beverages	277,720
	Net profit	52,640
Unit 8	Sales	640,500
	Gross profit food and beverages	416,325
	Net profit	80,063

YEAR ENDING 1989 UNIT RESULTS

		£
Unit 9	Sales	495,600
	Gross profit food and beverages	341,964
	Net profit	56,994
Unit 10	Sales	601,380
	Gross profit food and beverages	402,925
	Net profit	76,375
Unit 11	Sales	596,300
	Gross profit food and beverages	375,669
	Net profit	67,084
Unit 12	Sales	637,600
	Gross profit food and beverages	385,748
	Net profit	82,888
Unit 13	Sales	549,300
	Gross profit food and beverages	318,594
	Net profit	53,557
Unit 14	Sales	713,000
	Gross profit food and beverages	420,670
	Net profit	67,735
Unit 15	Sales	639,000
	Gross profit food and beverages	421,740
	Net profit	70,290

TRADING AND PROFIT AND LOSS ACCOUNT
TO 31 MARCH 1990.

		£
Sales		9,470,040
Less Cost of sales	3,475,735	
Gross profit		5,994,305
Less		
Labour	2,851,957	
Salaries	336,751	
Incentive bonuses	45,949	
Other department operating expenses	213,750	
Undistributed operating expenses		
Administration and general	75,600	
Marketing	461,041	
Energy	476,596	
Property operation and maintenance	27,600	
Painting and decorating	39,760	
Fixed charges		
Insurance	187,061	
Depreciation	46,865	
Rates	131,396	
Rent	11,340	
		1,090,639